Cane
libro da colorare

Coloring Pages for Kids

Coloring Pages for Kids
An imprint of Ciparum LLC

Cane libro da colorare
© 2017 Ciparum LLC
All rights reserved.
ISBN-10:1-63589-538-3
ISBN-13:978-1-63589-538-4

Coloring Pages for Kids

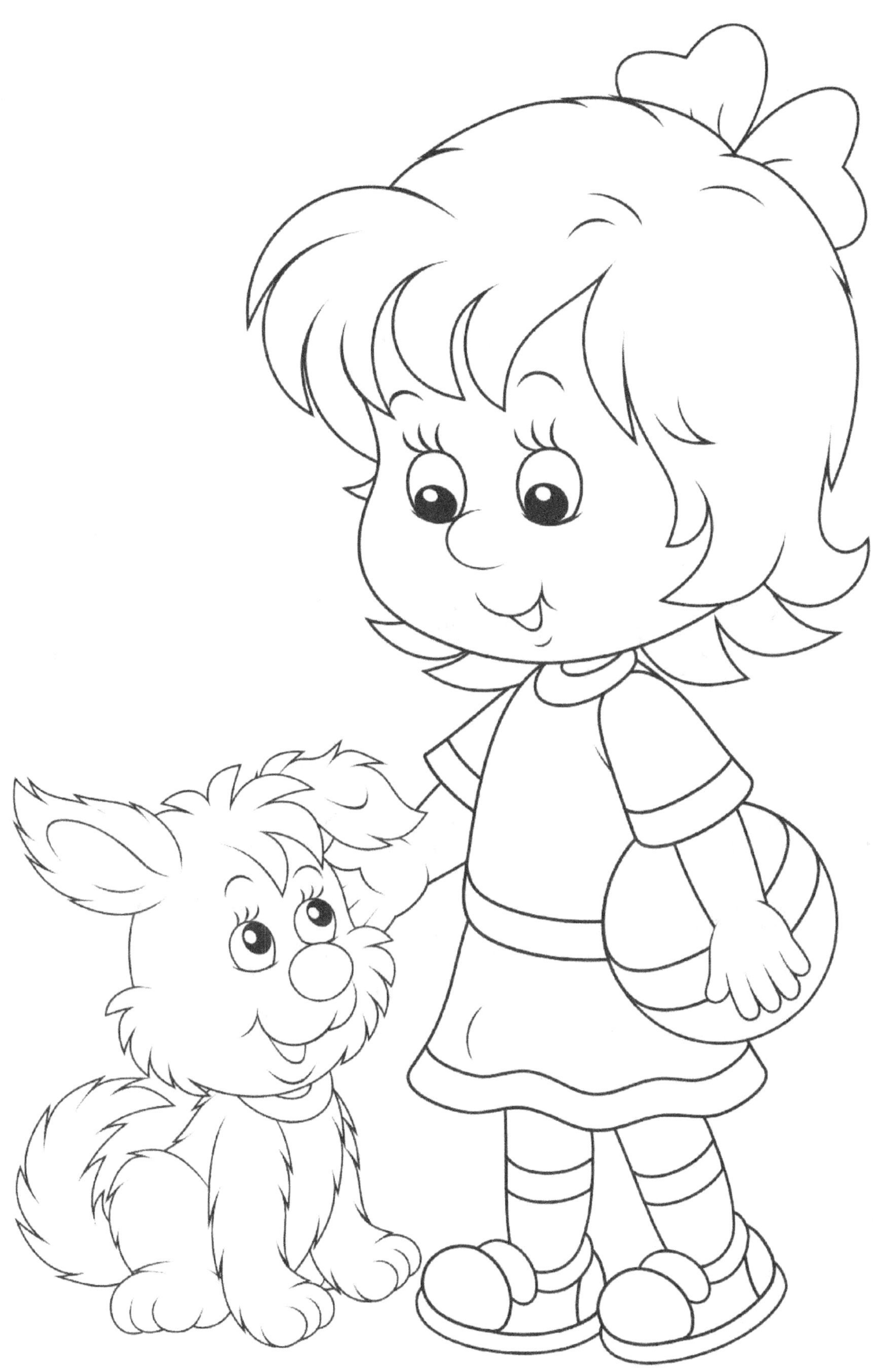

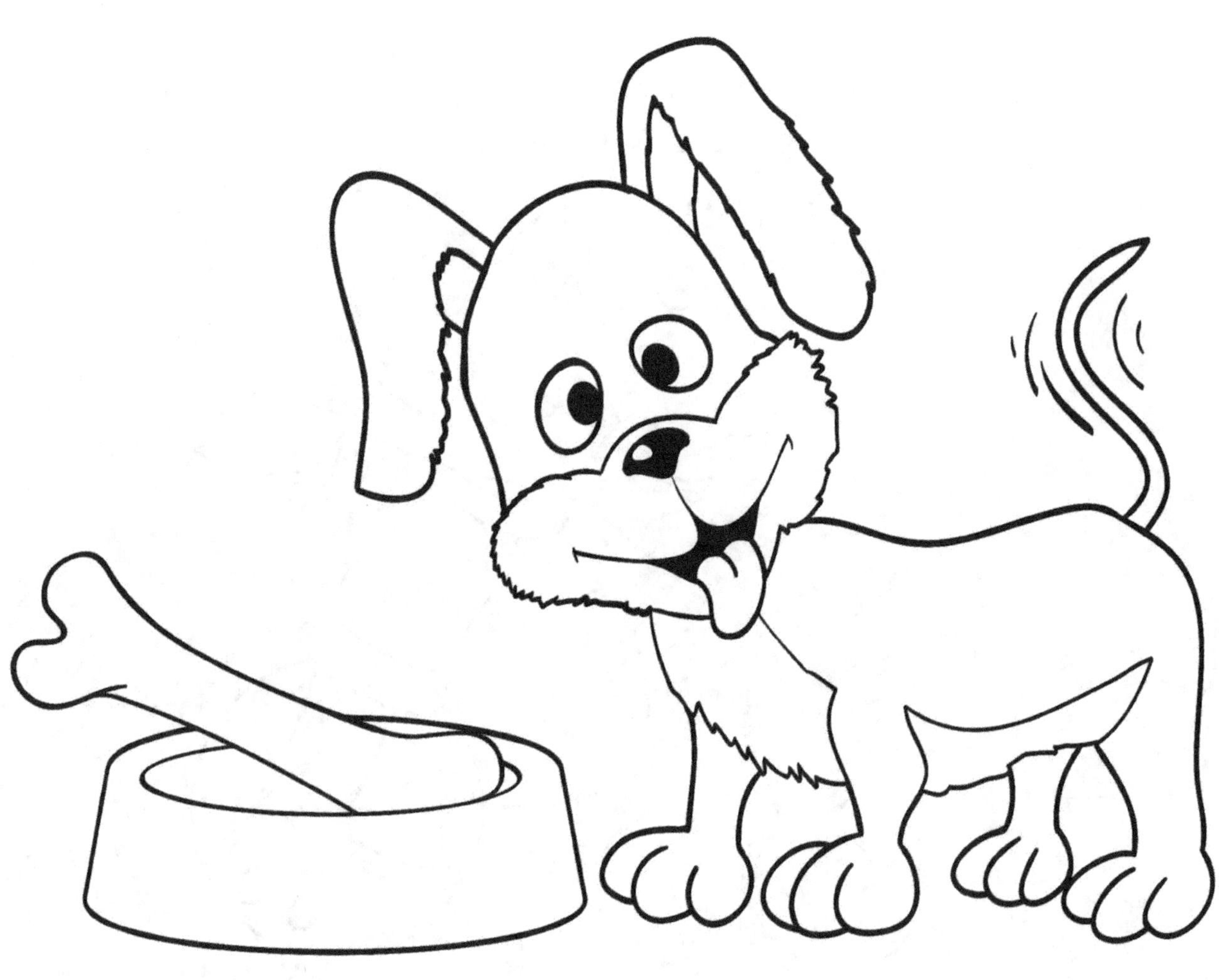

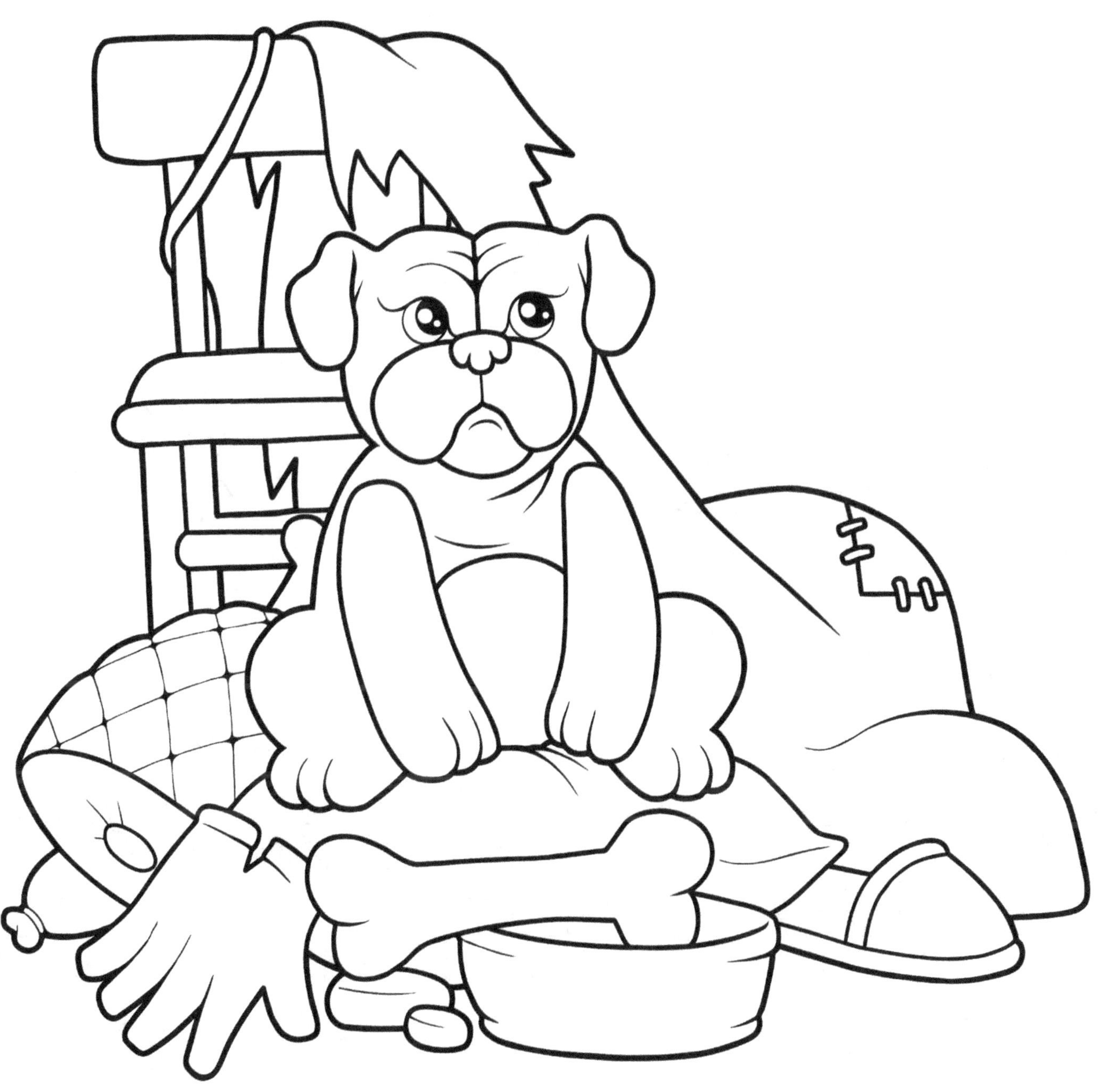

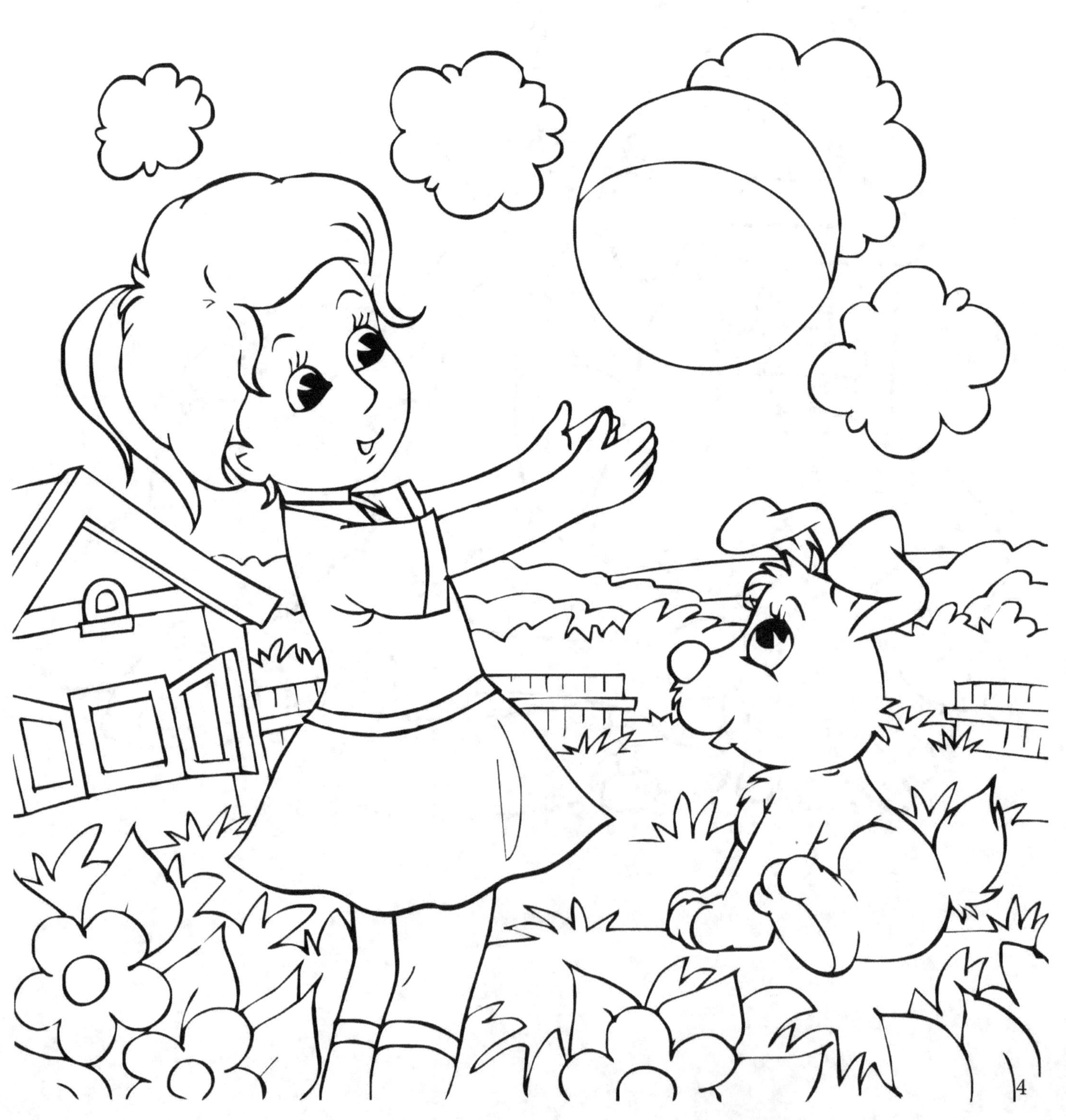

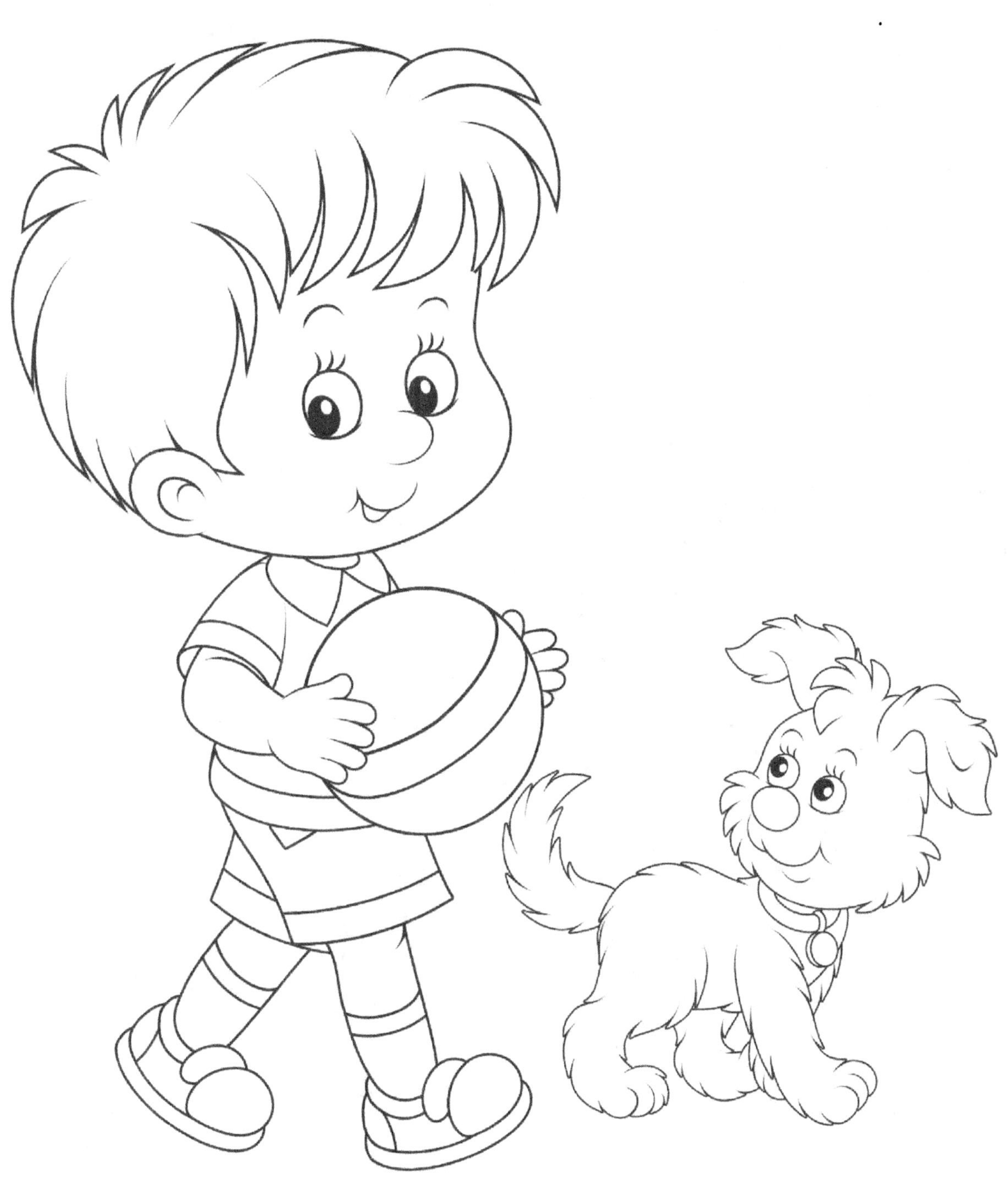

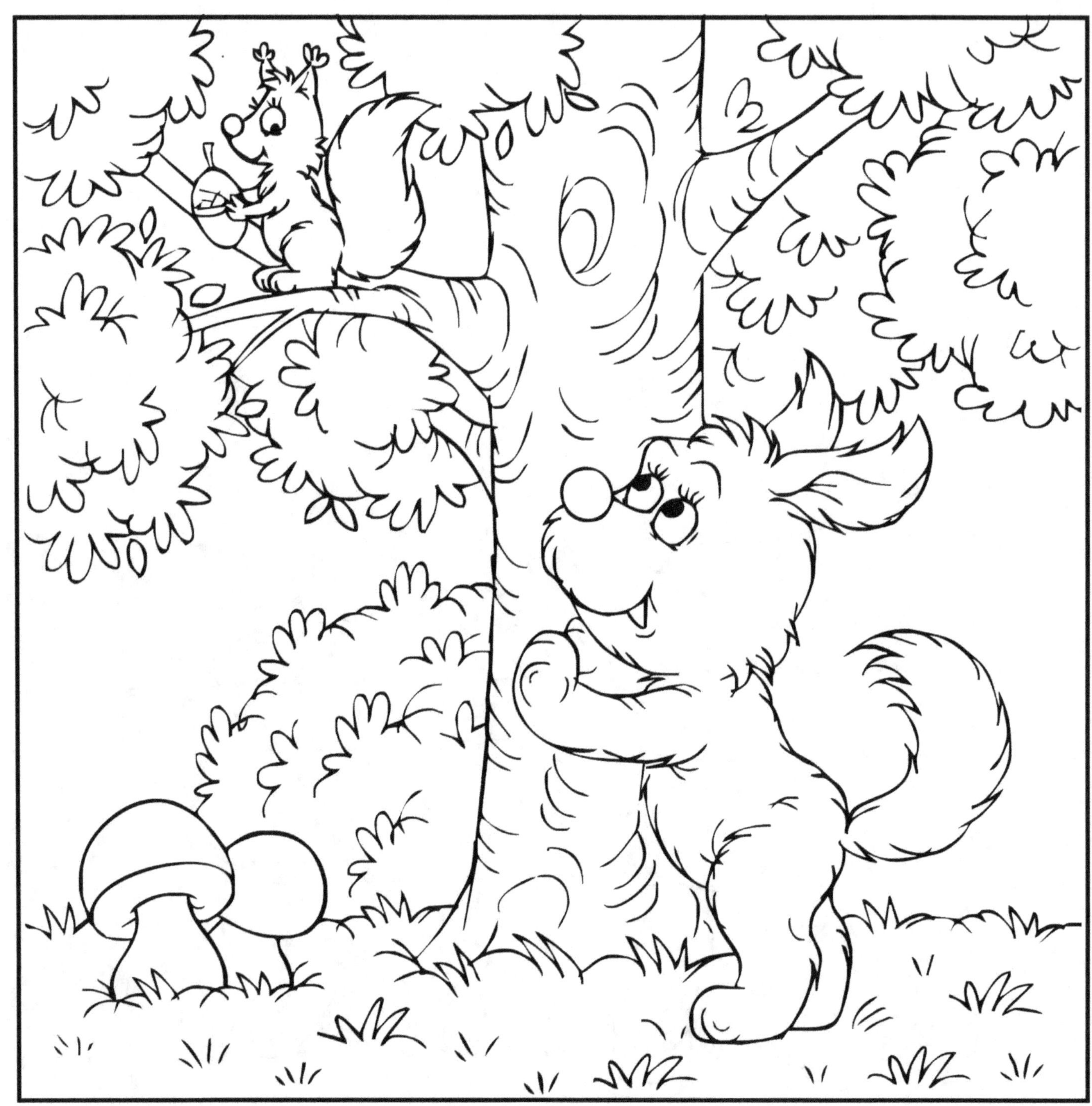

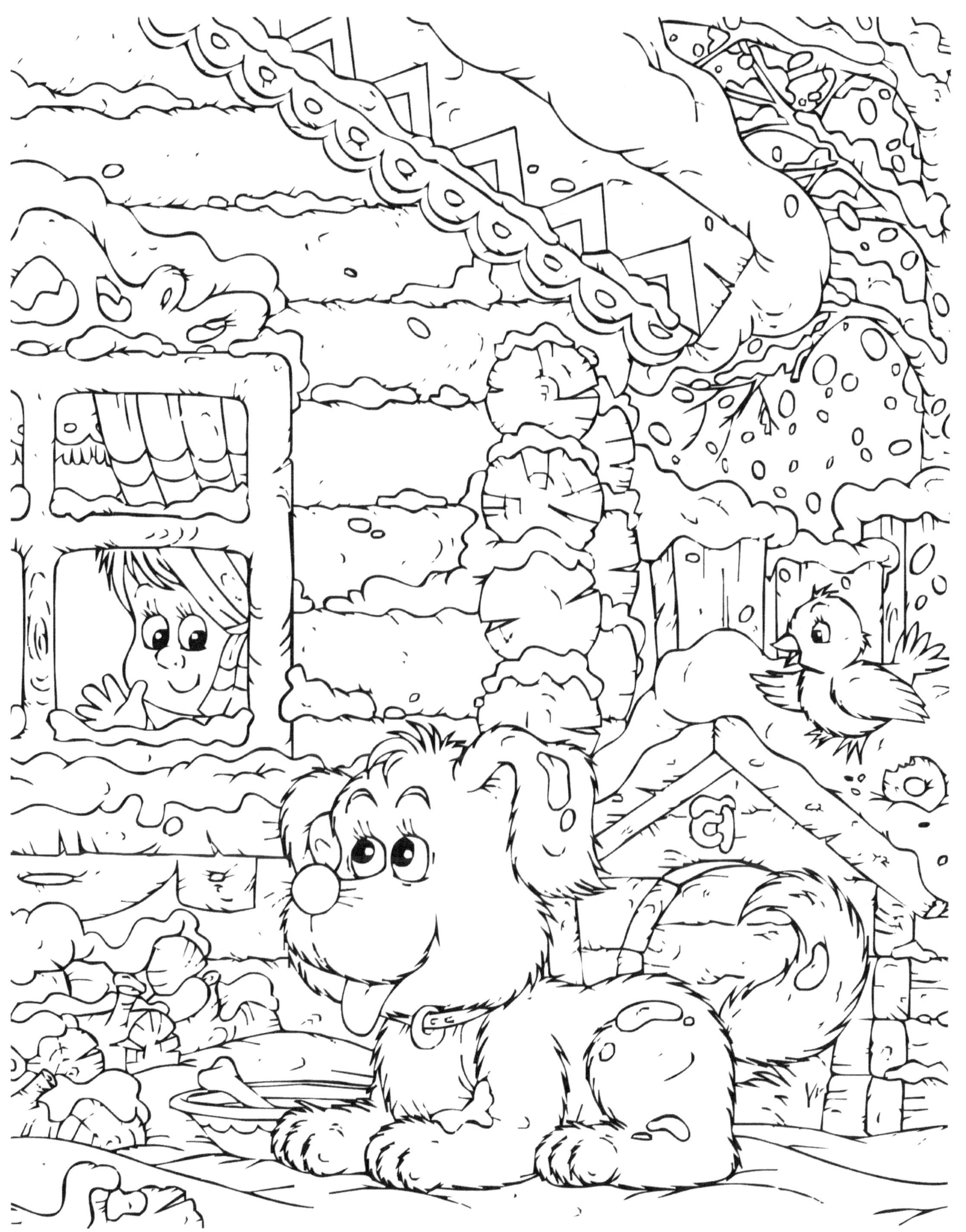

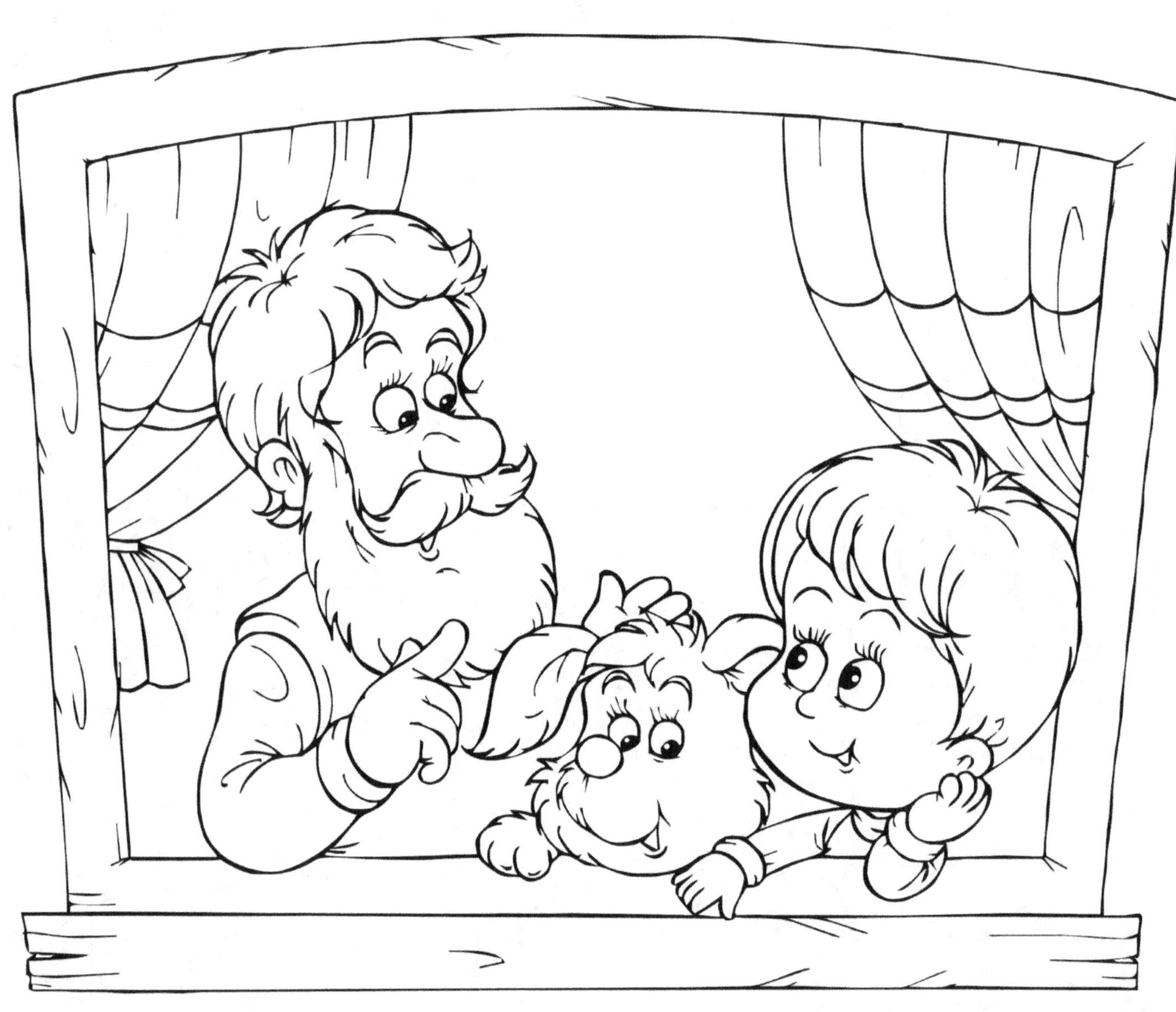

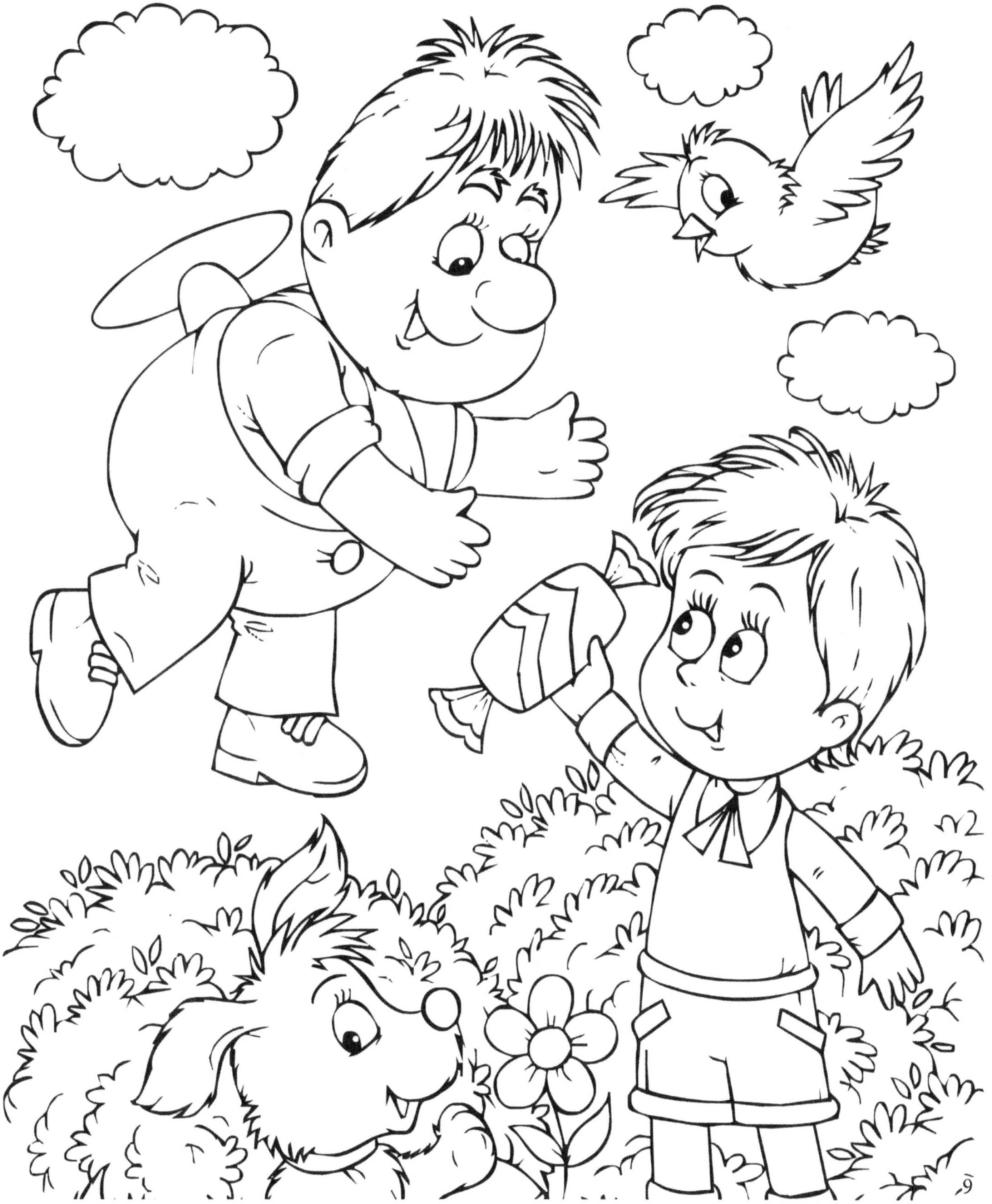

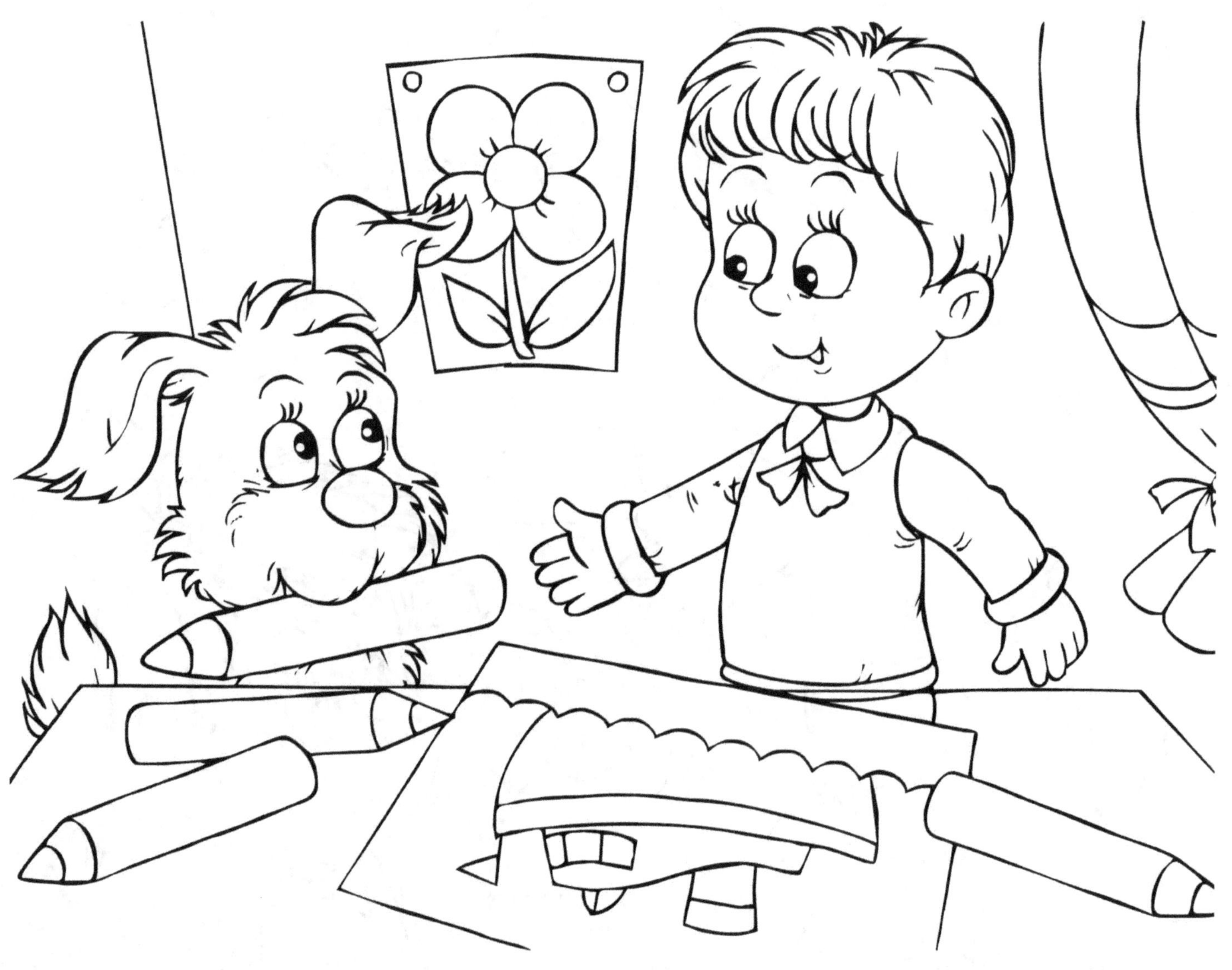

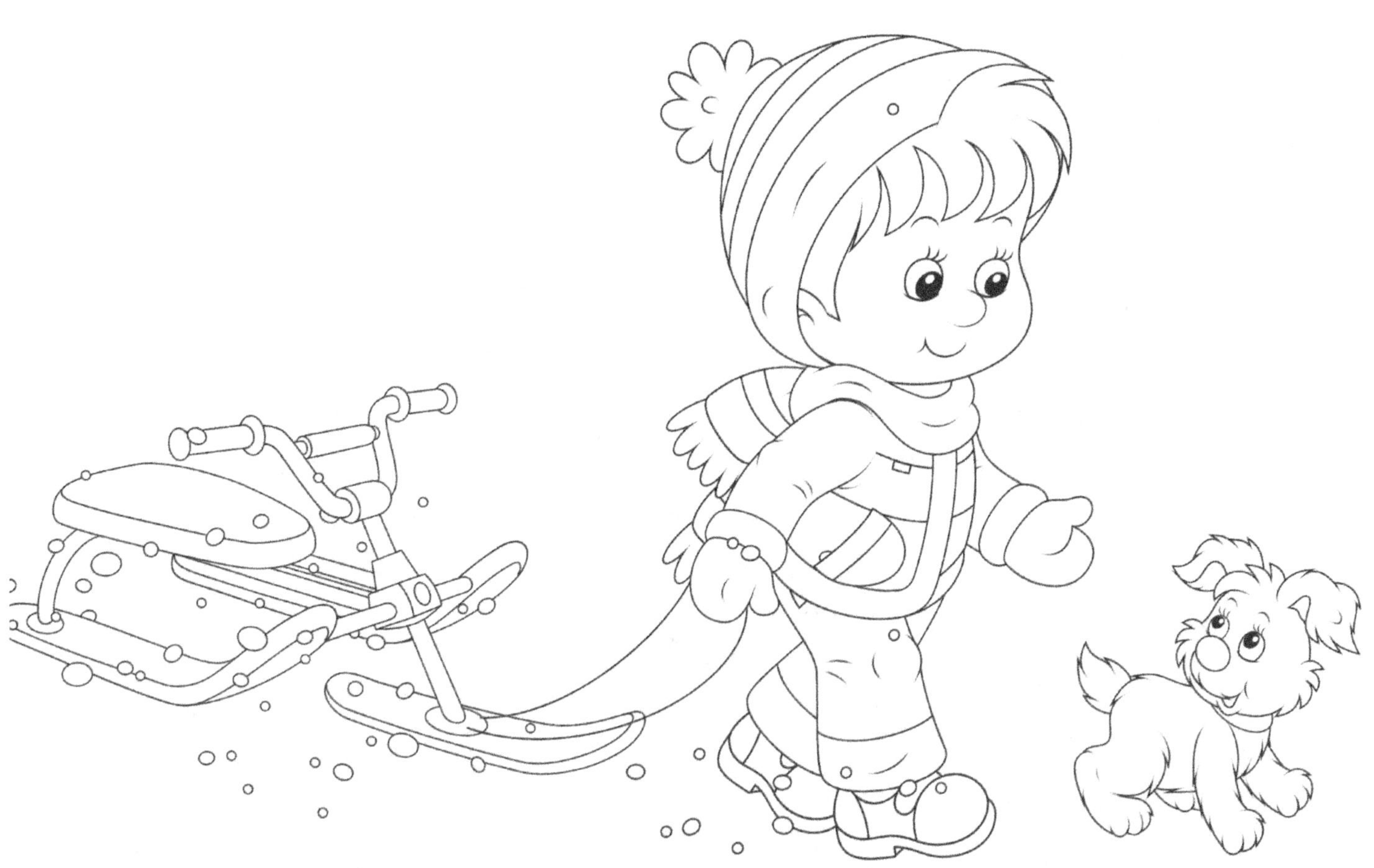

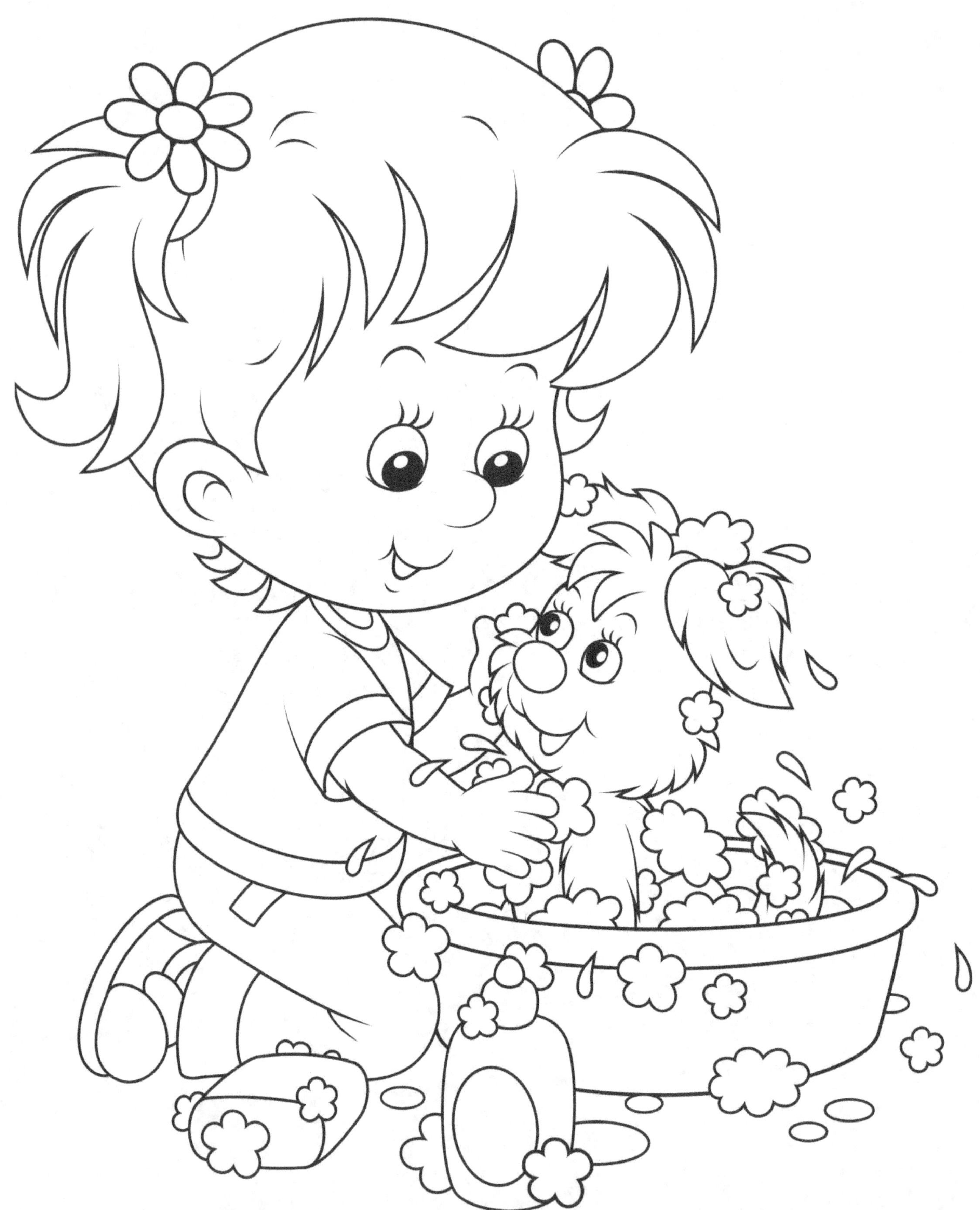

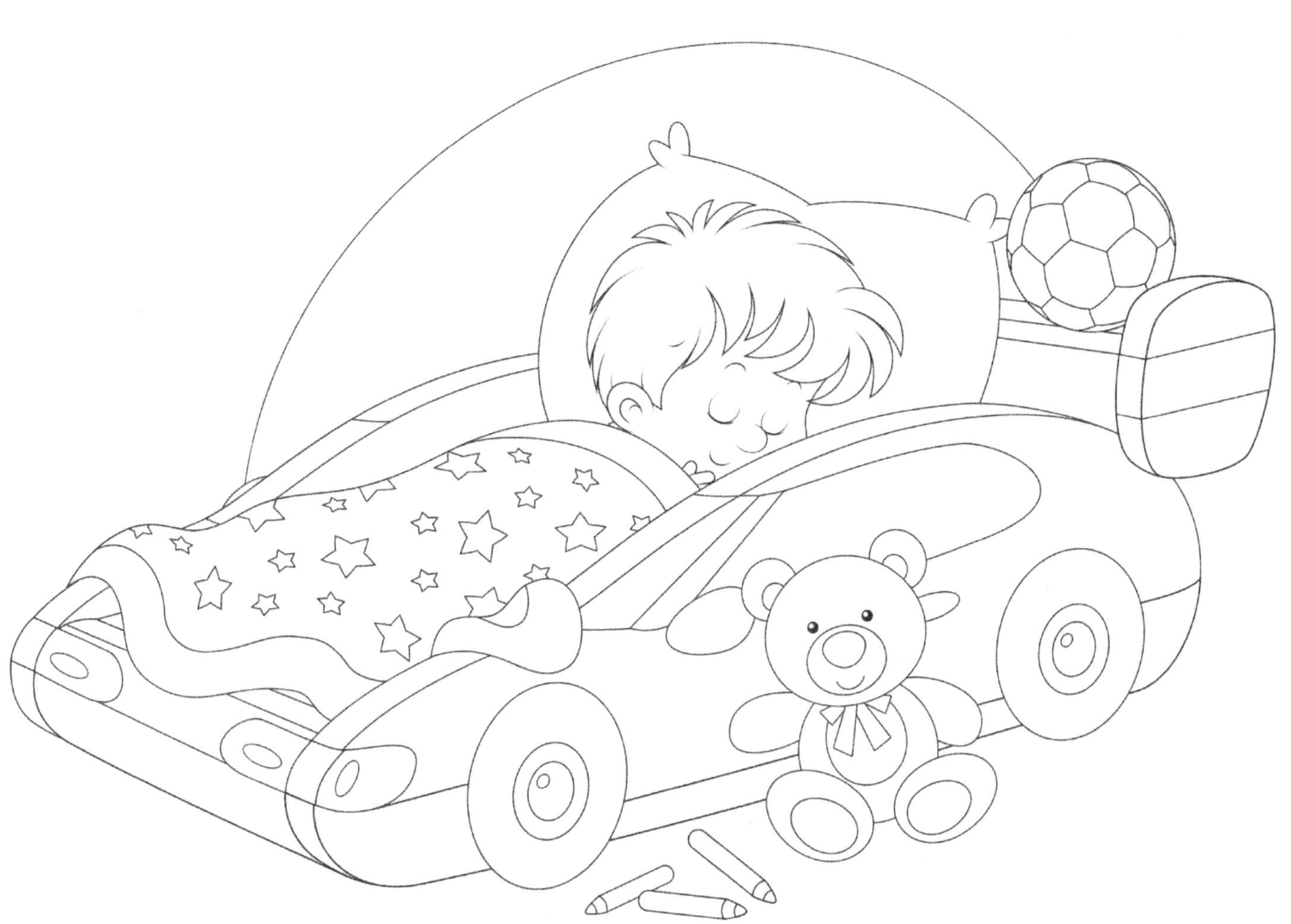

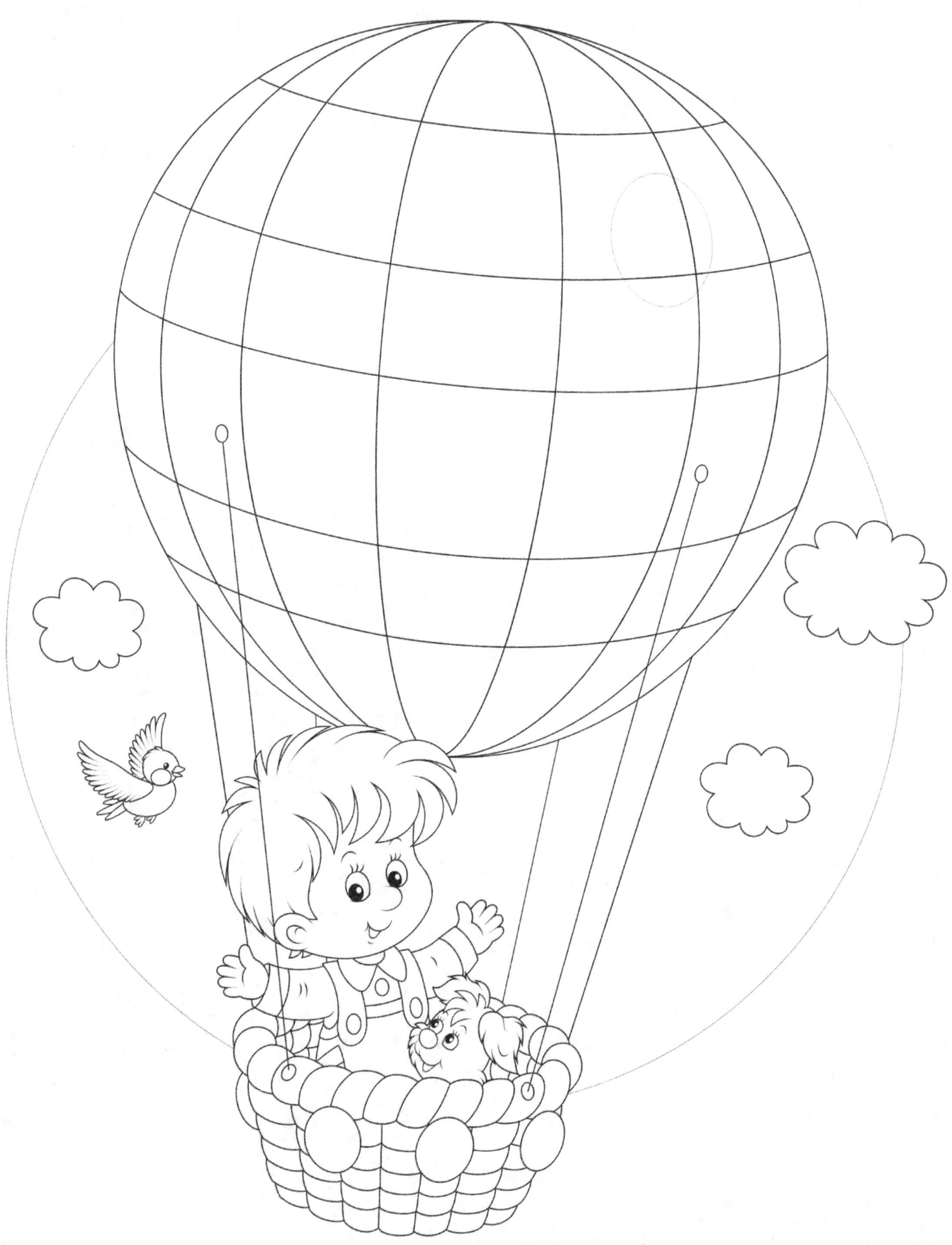

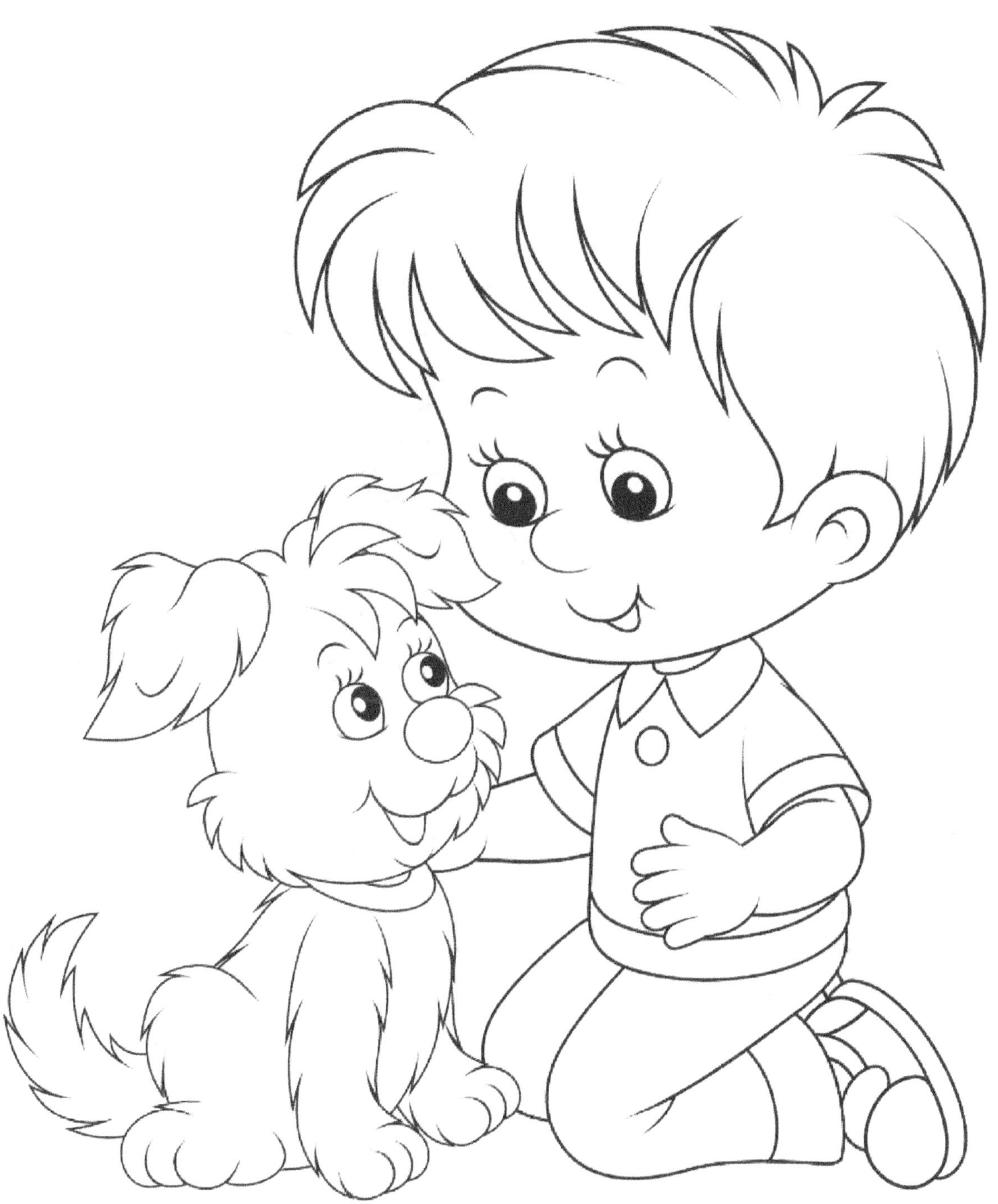

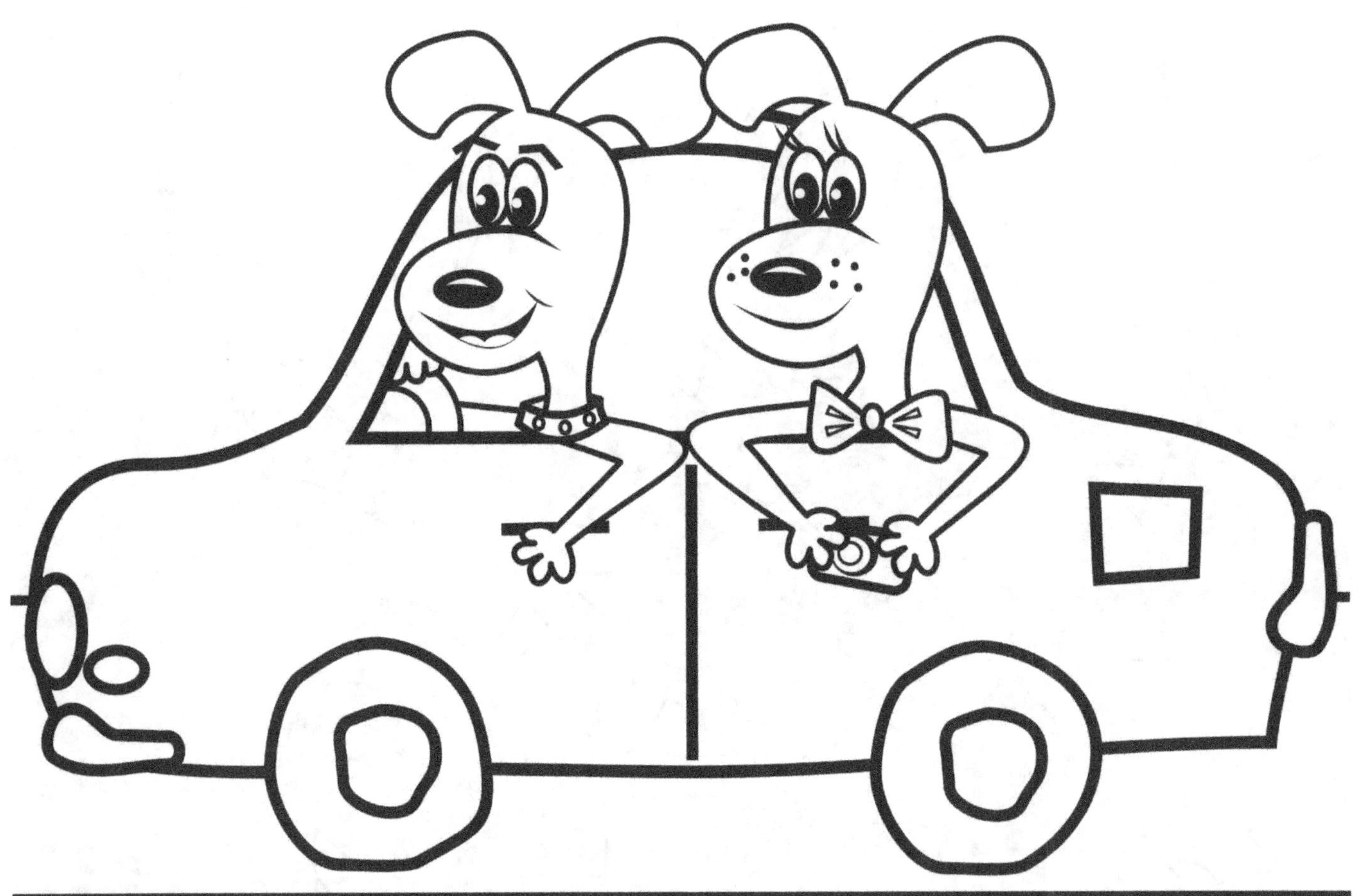

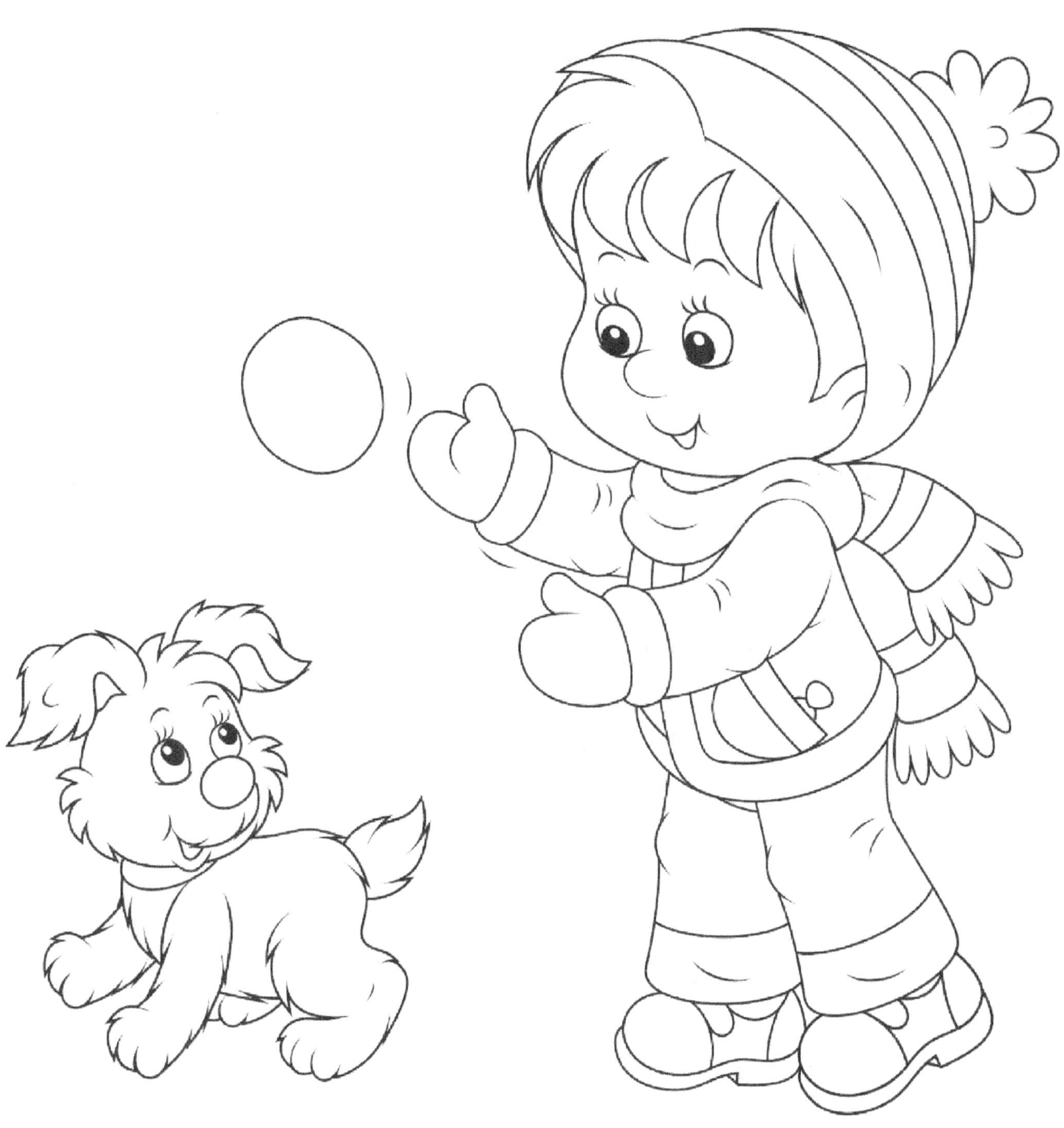

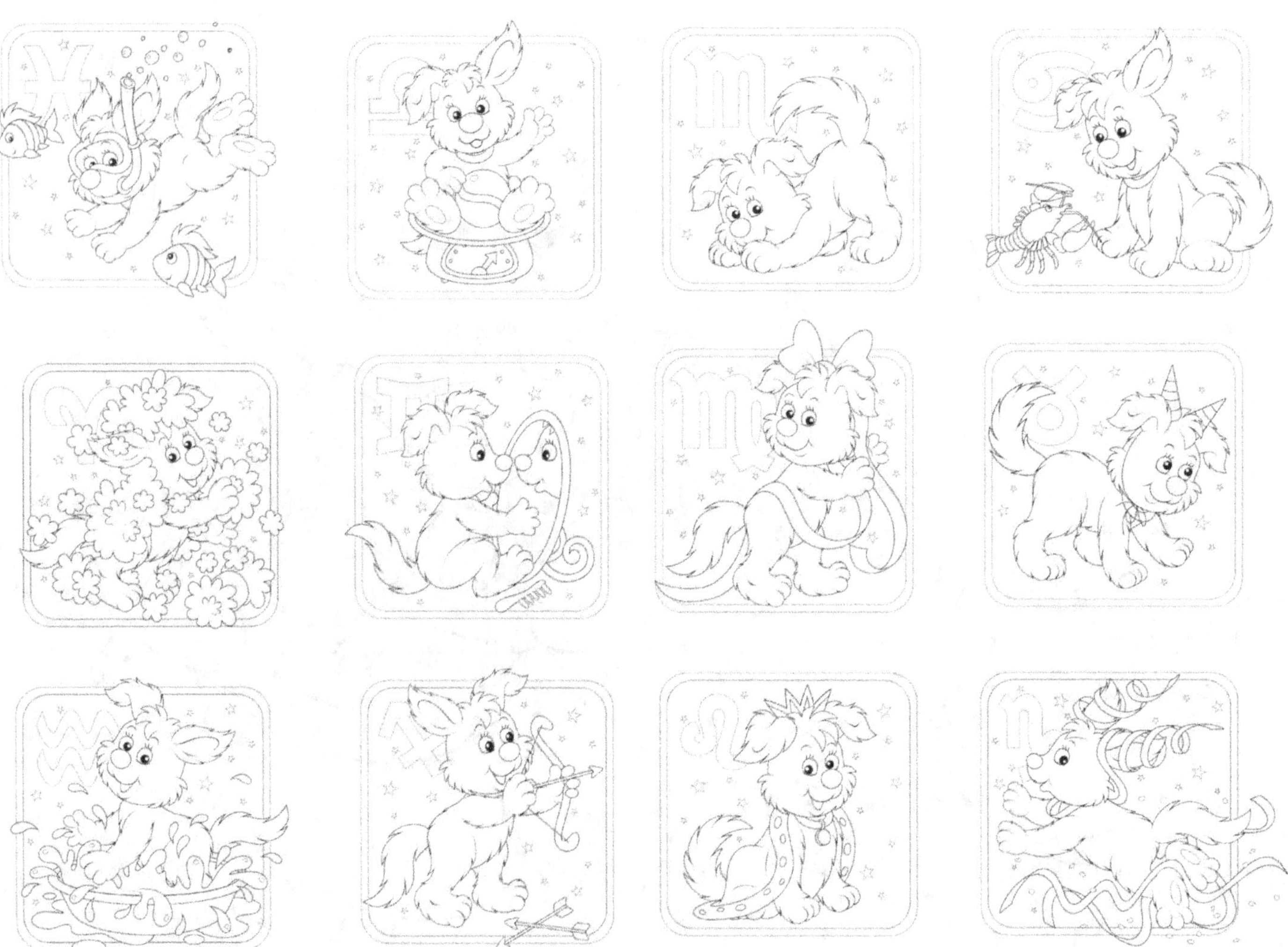

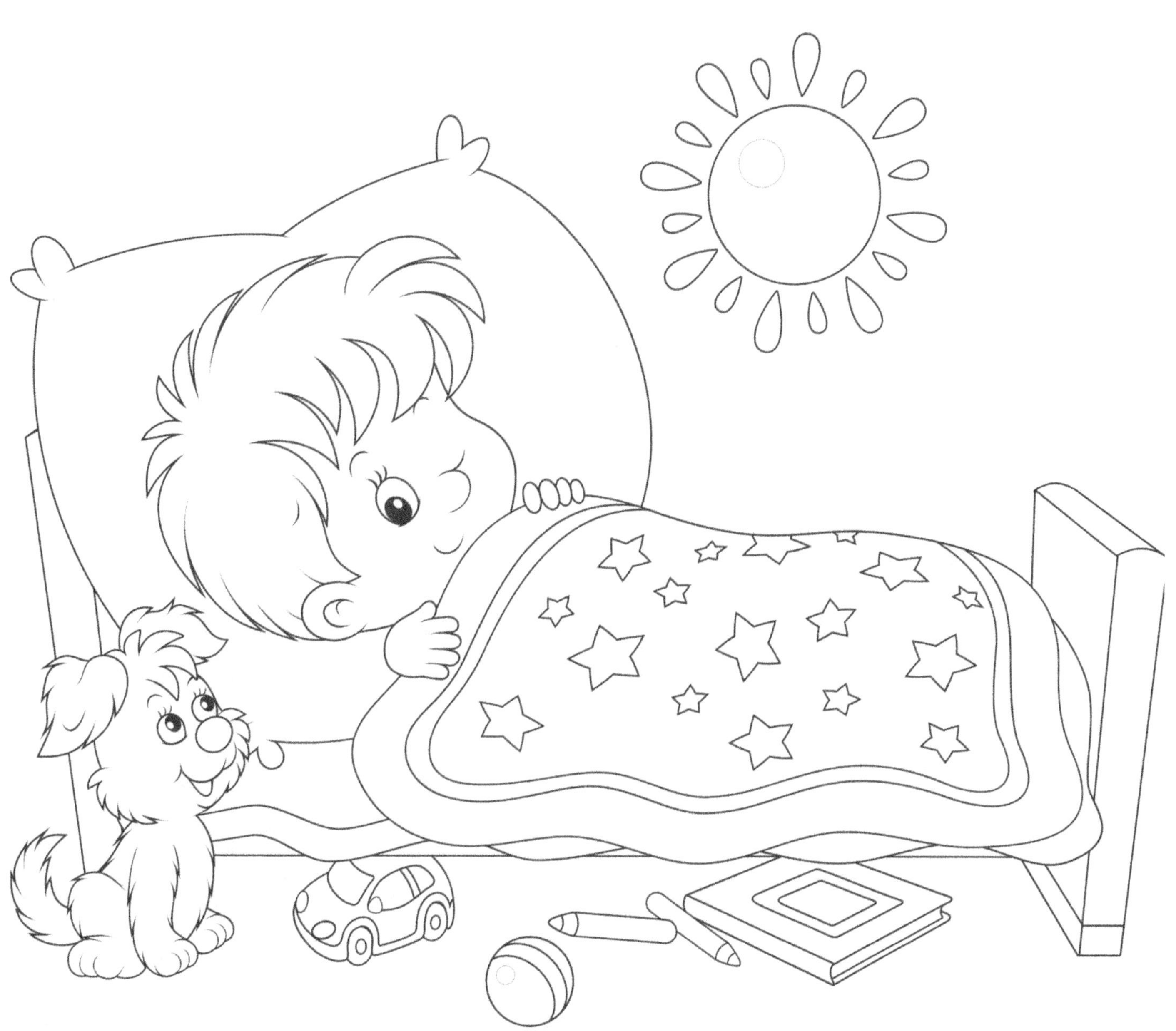

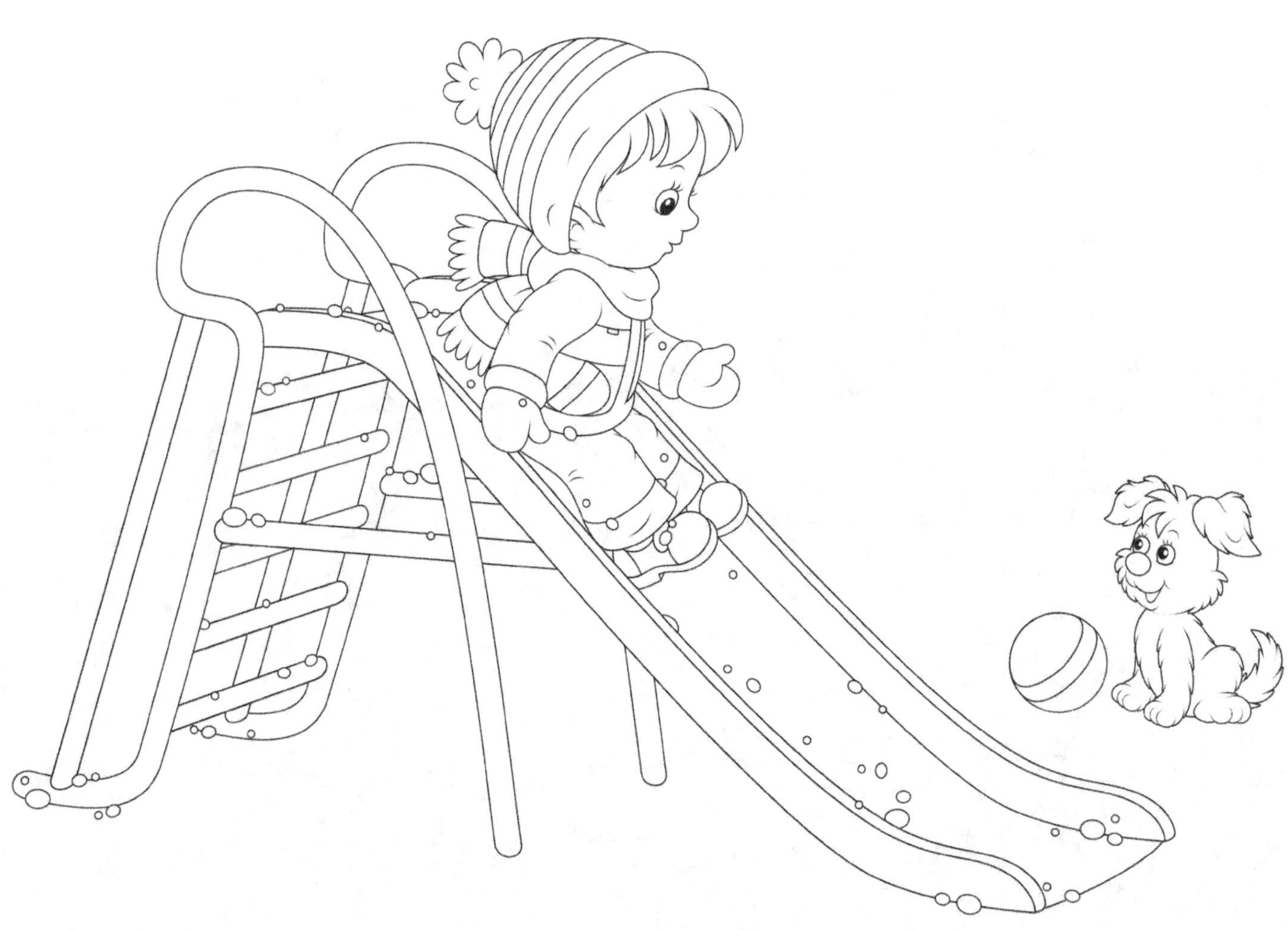

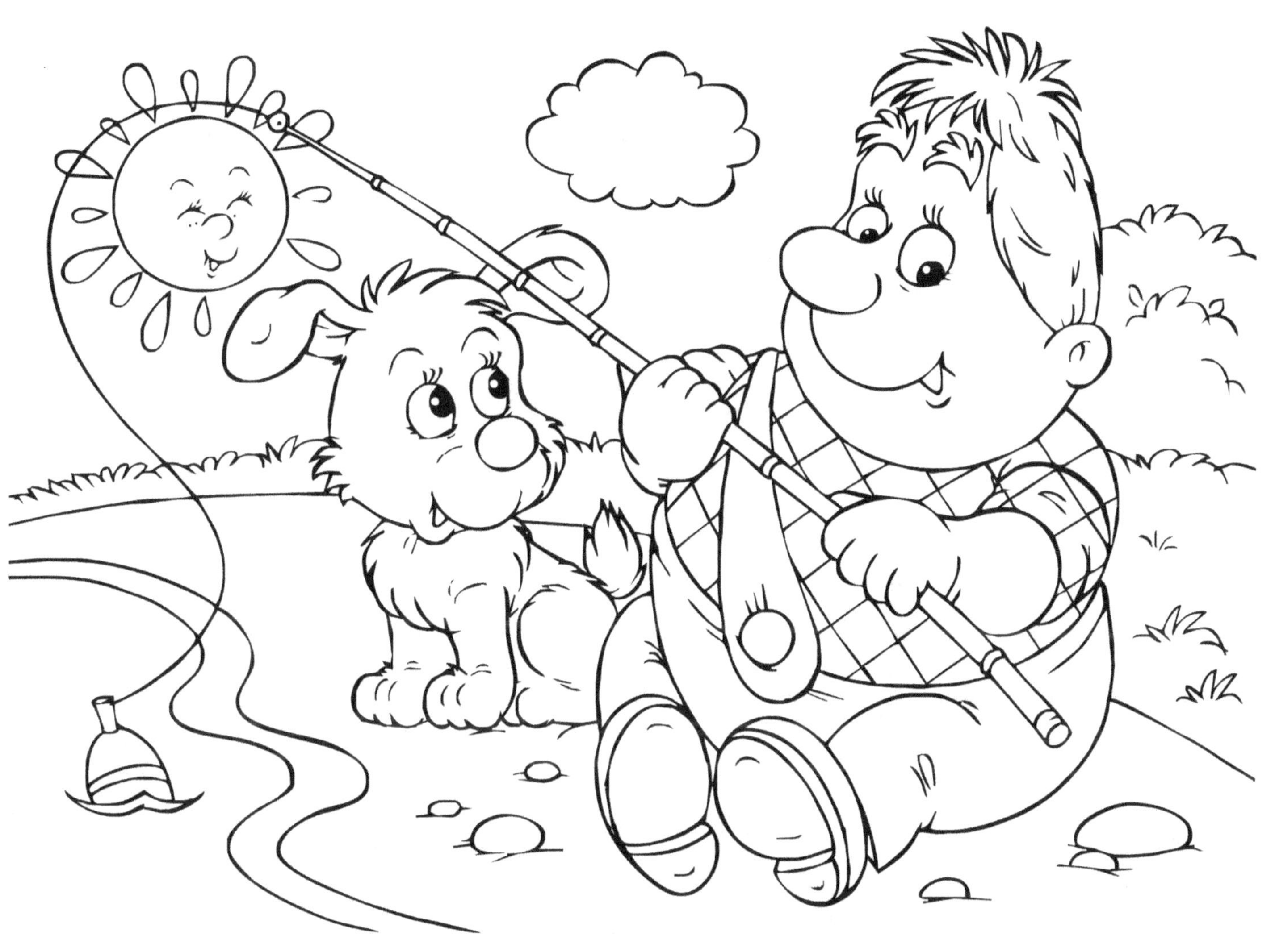

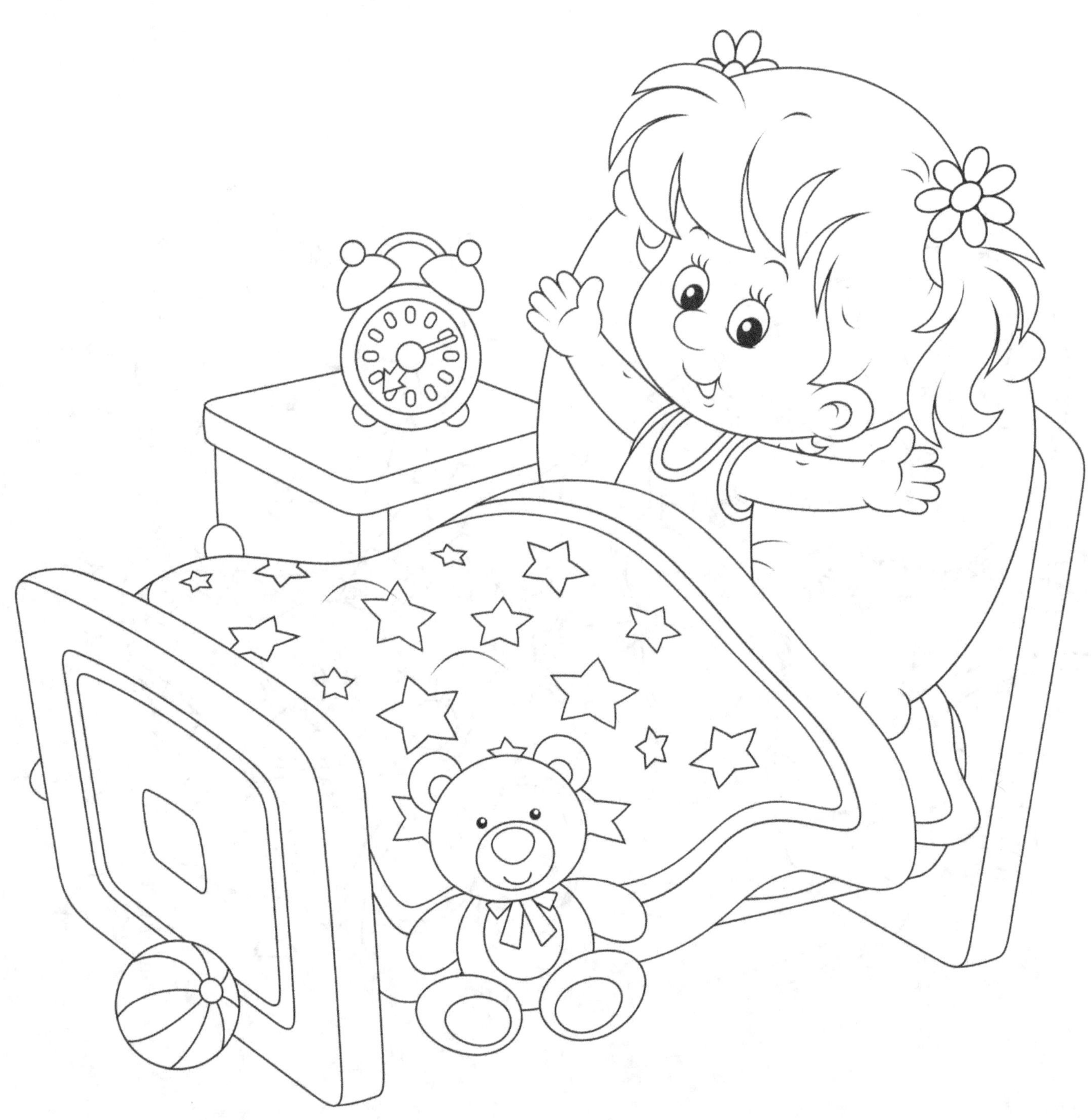

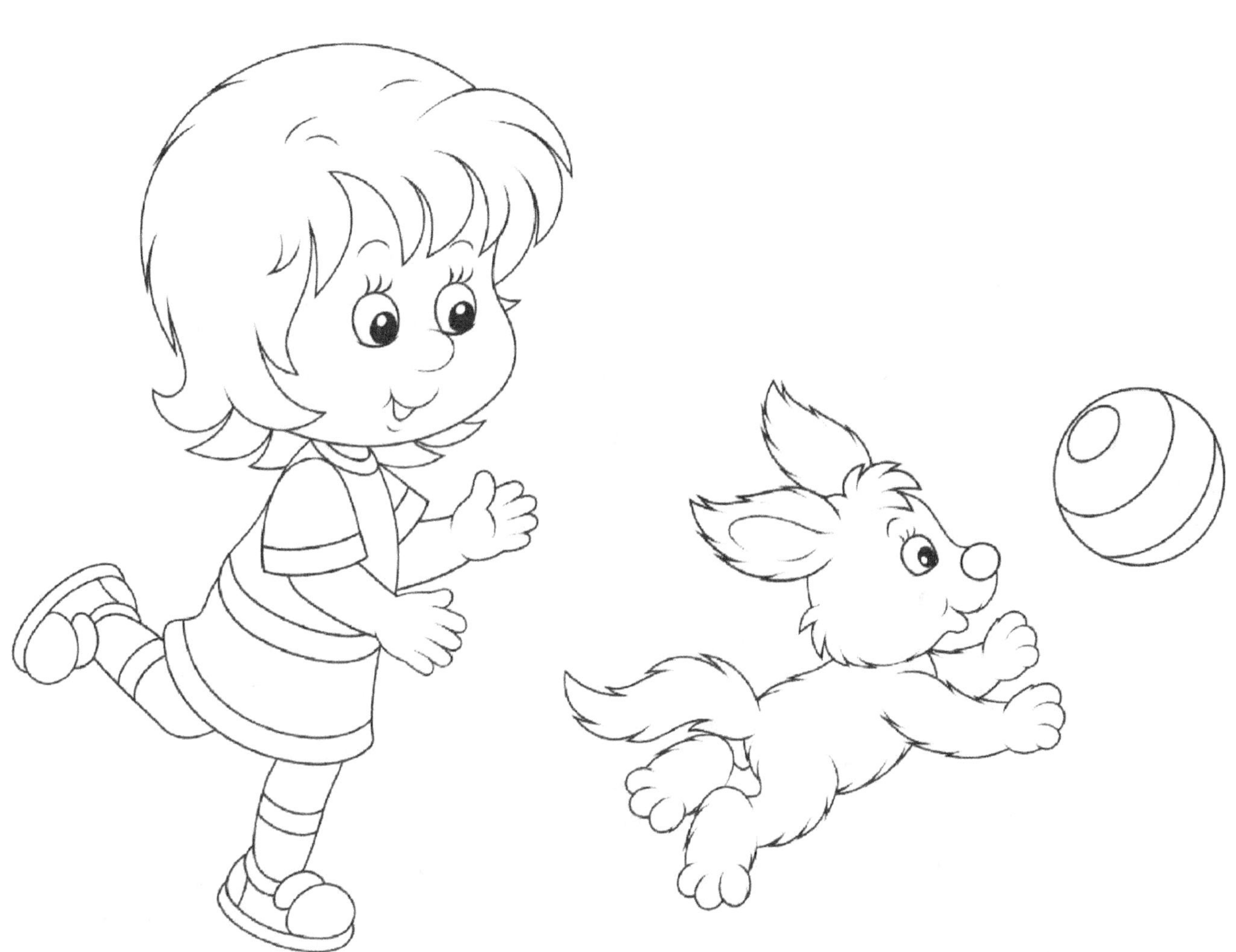

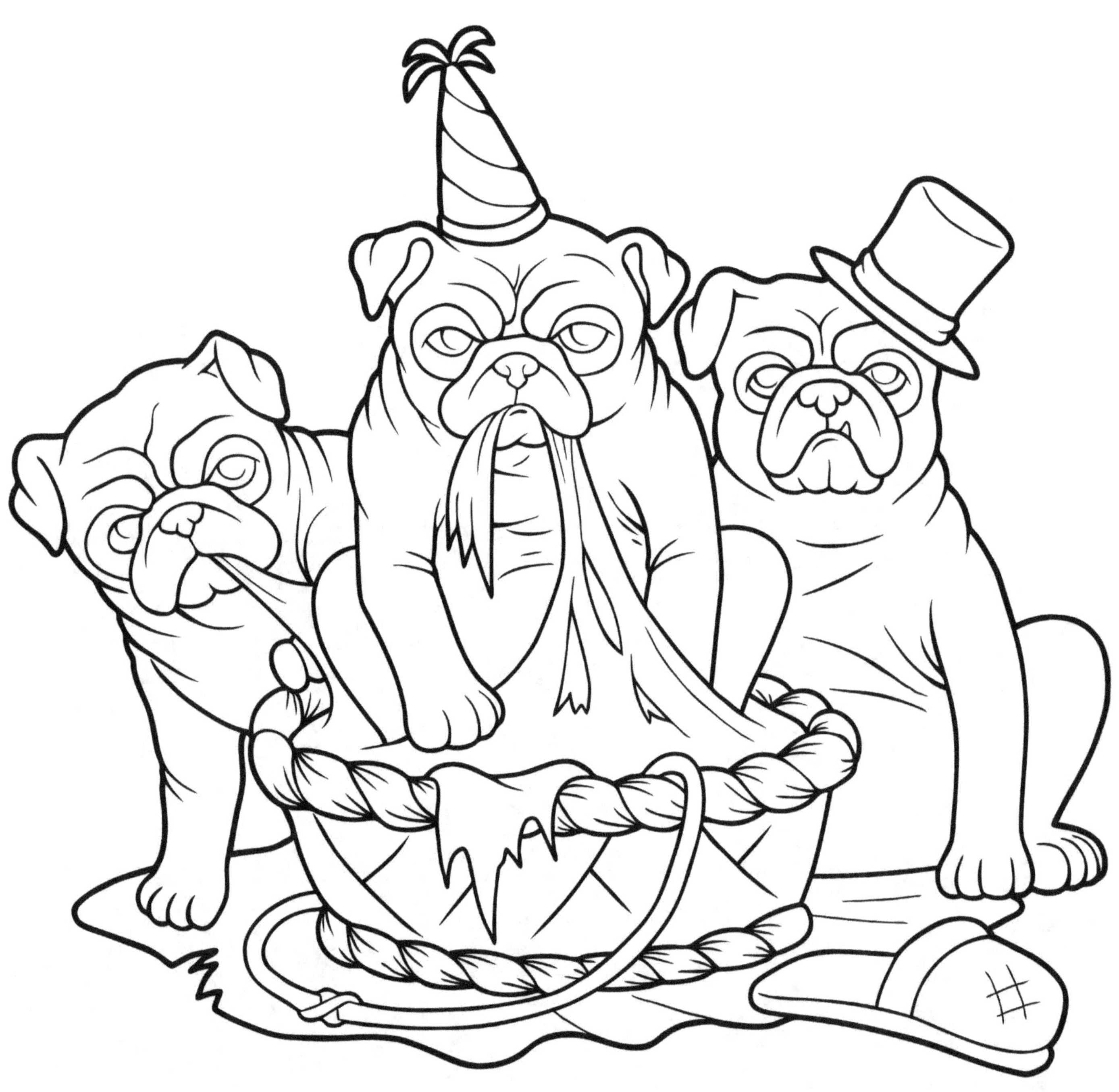

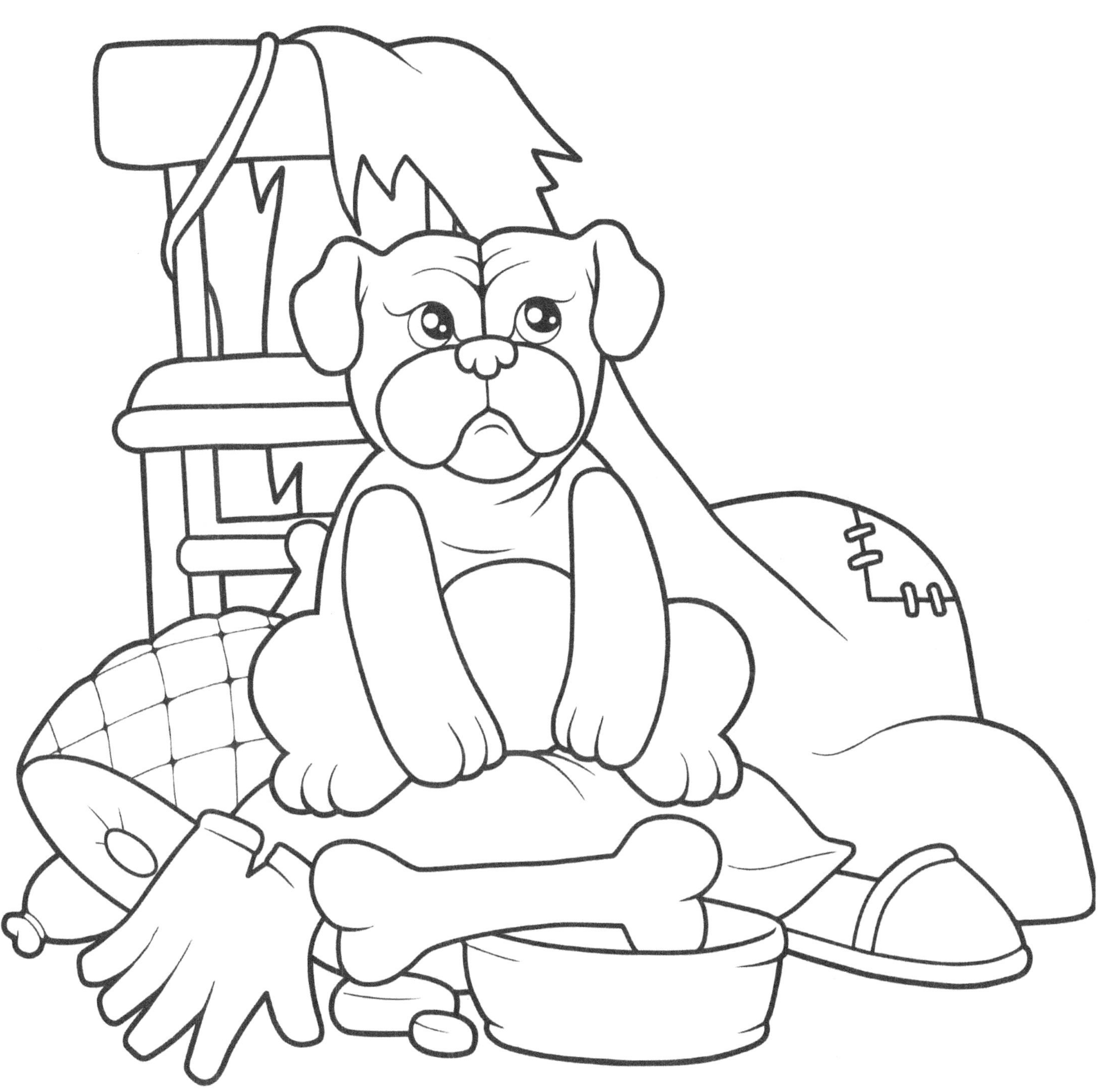

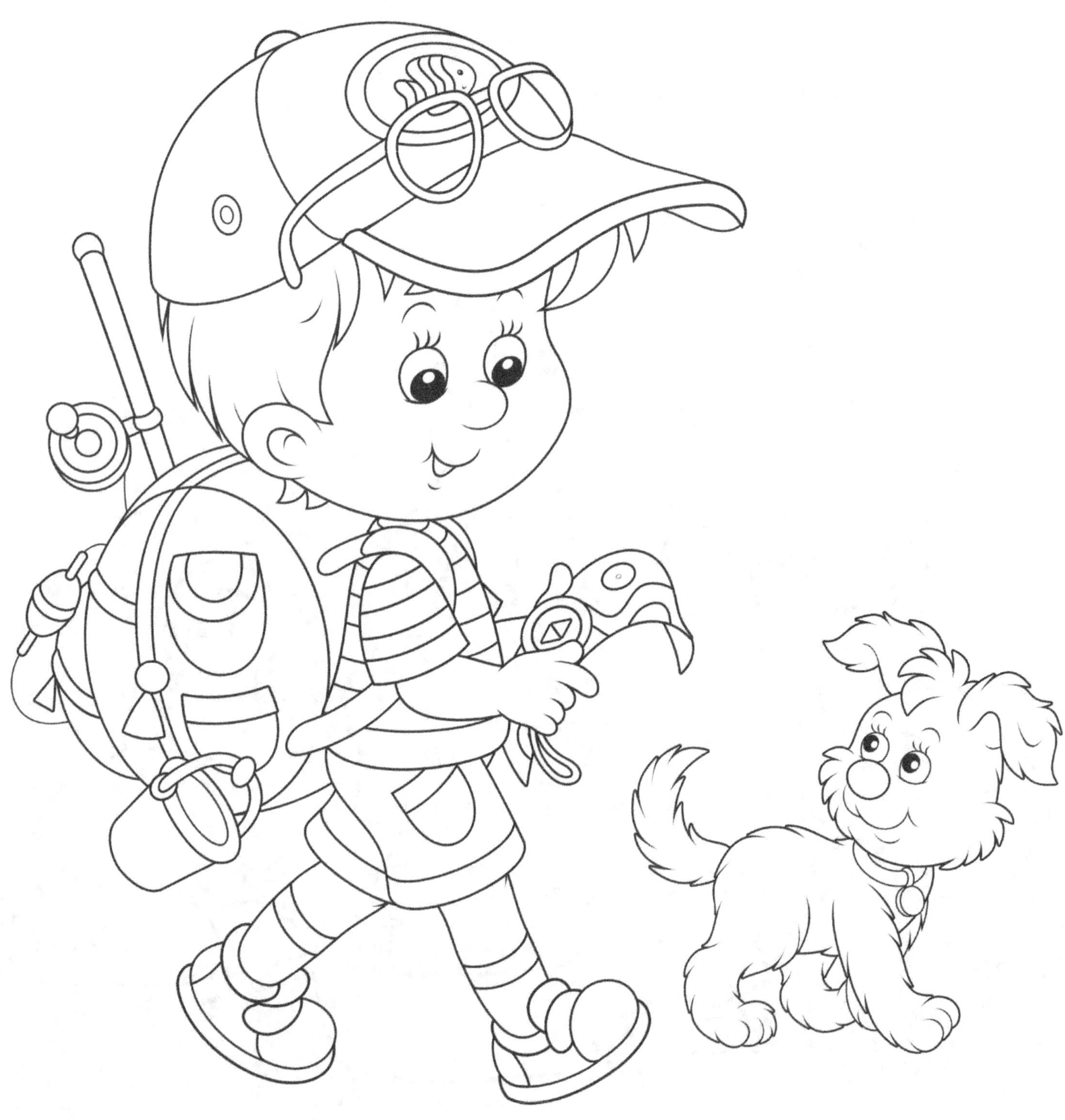

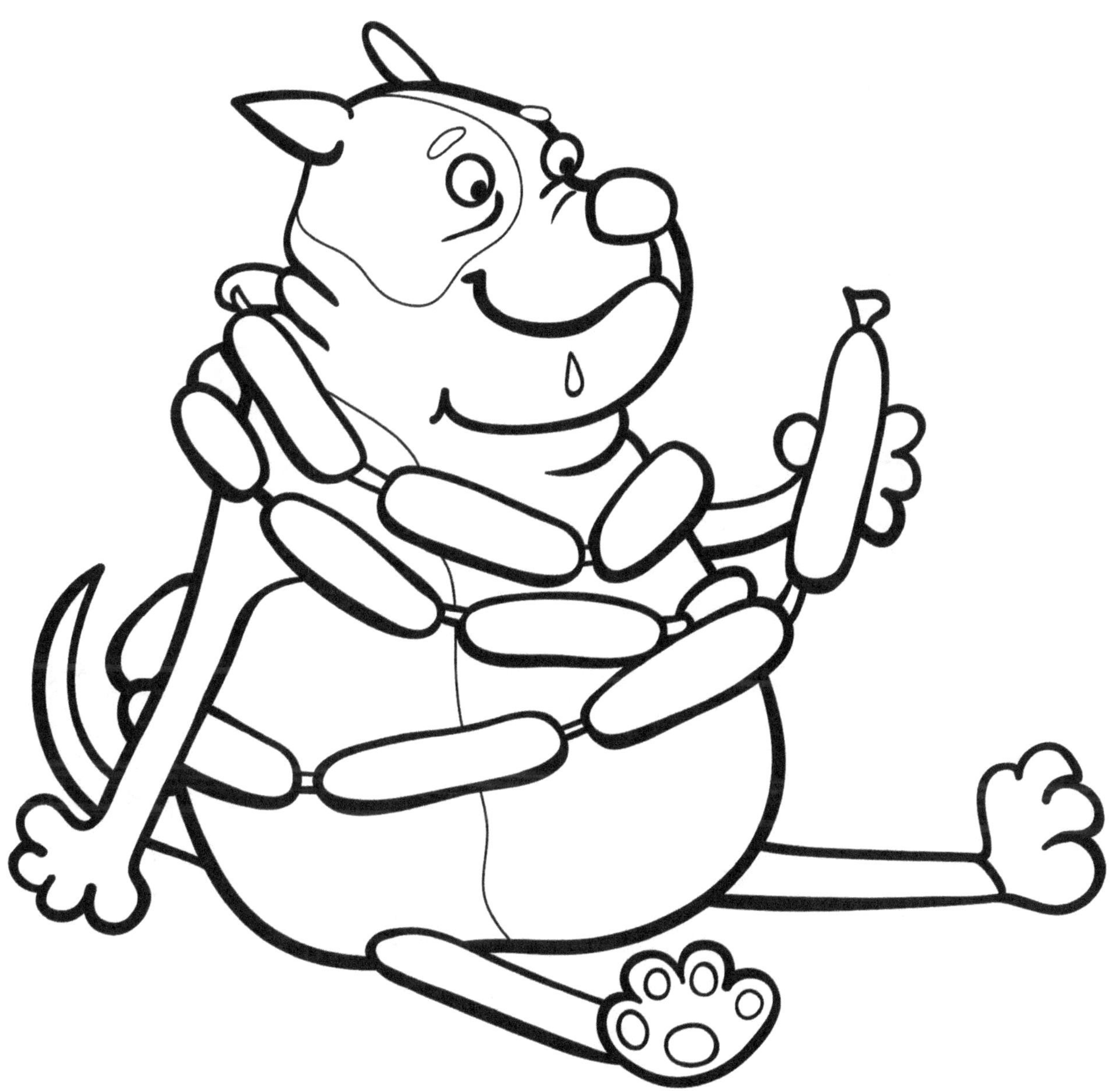

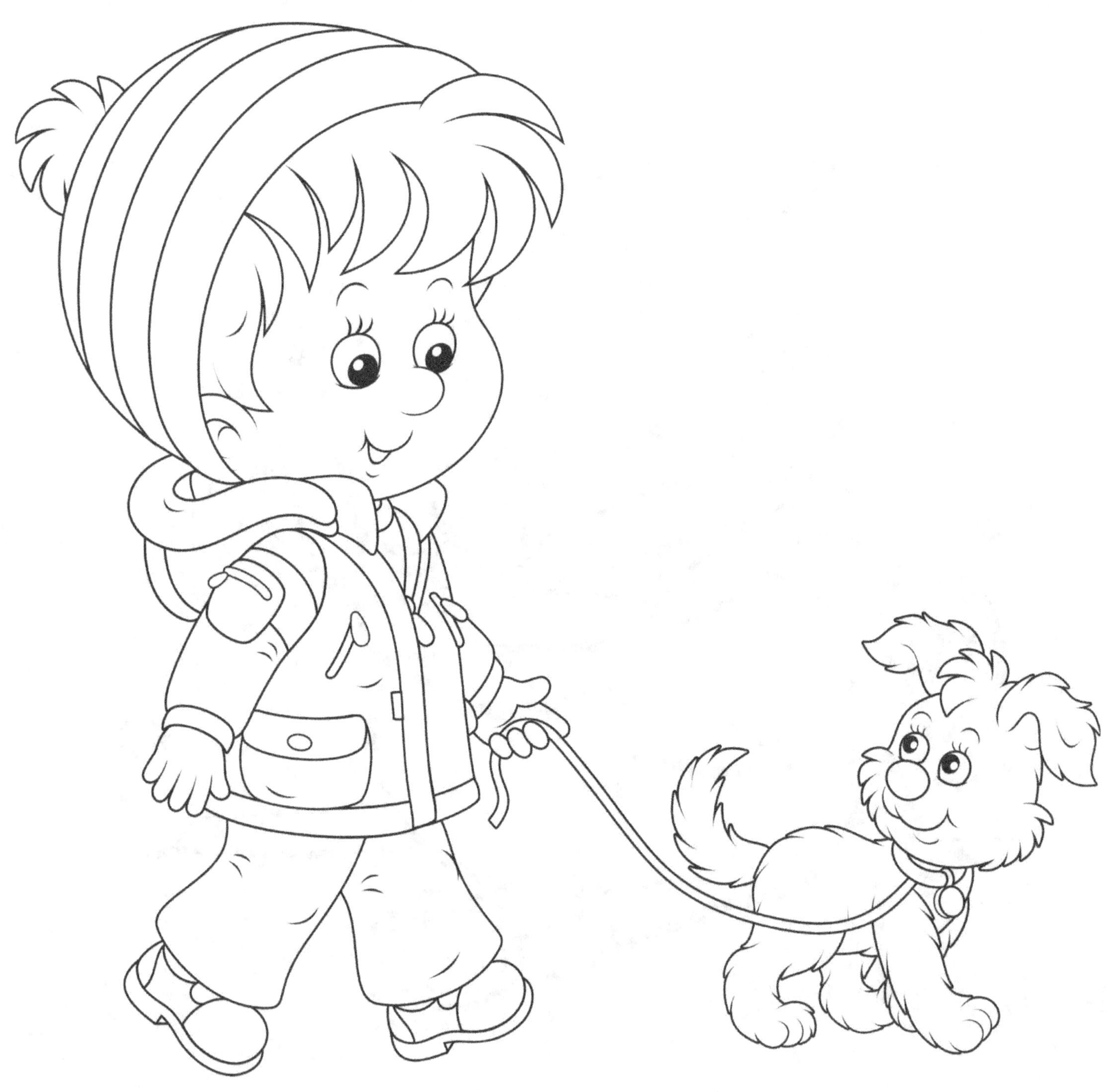

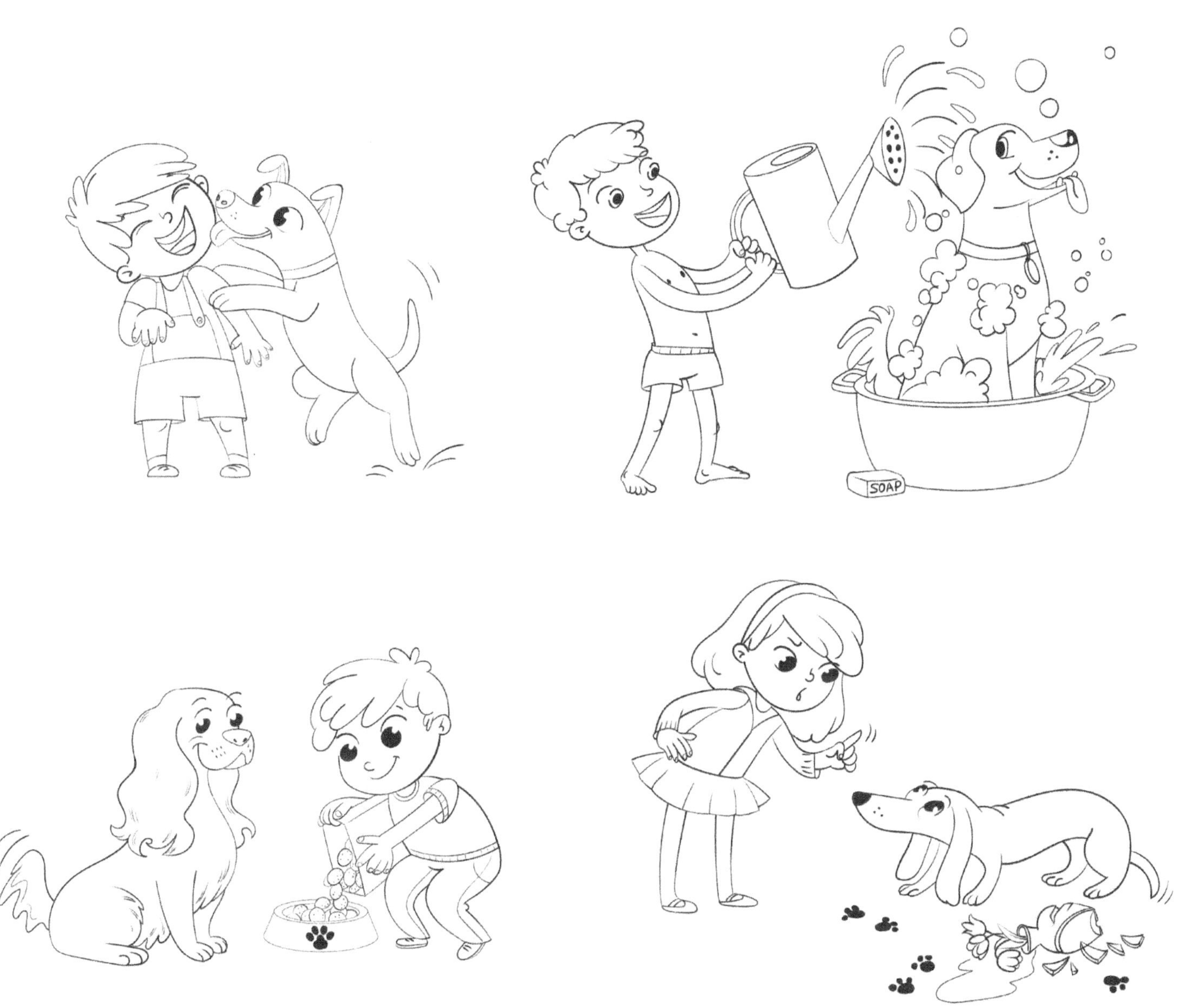

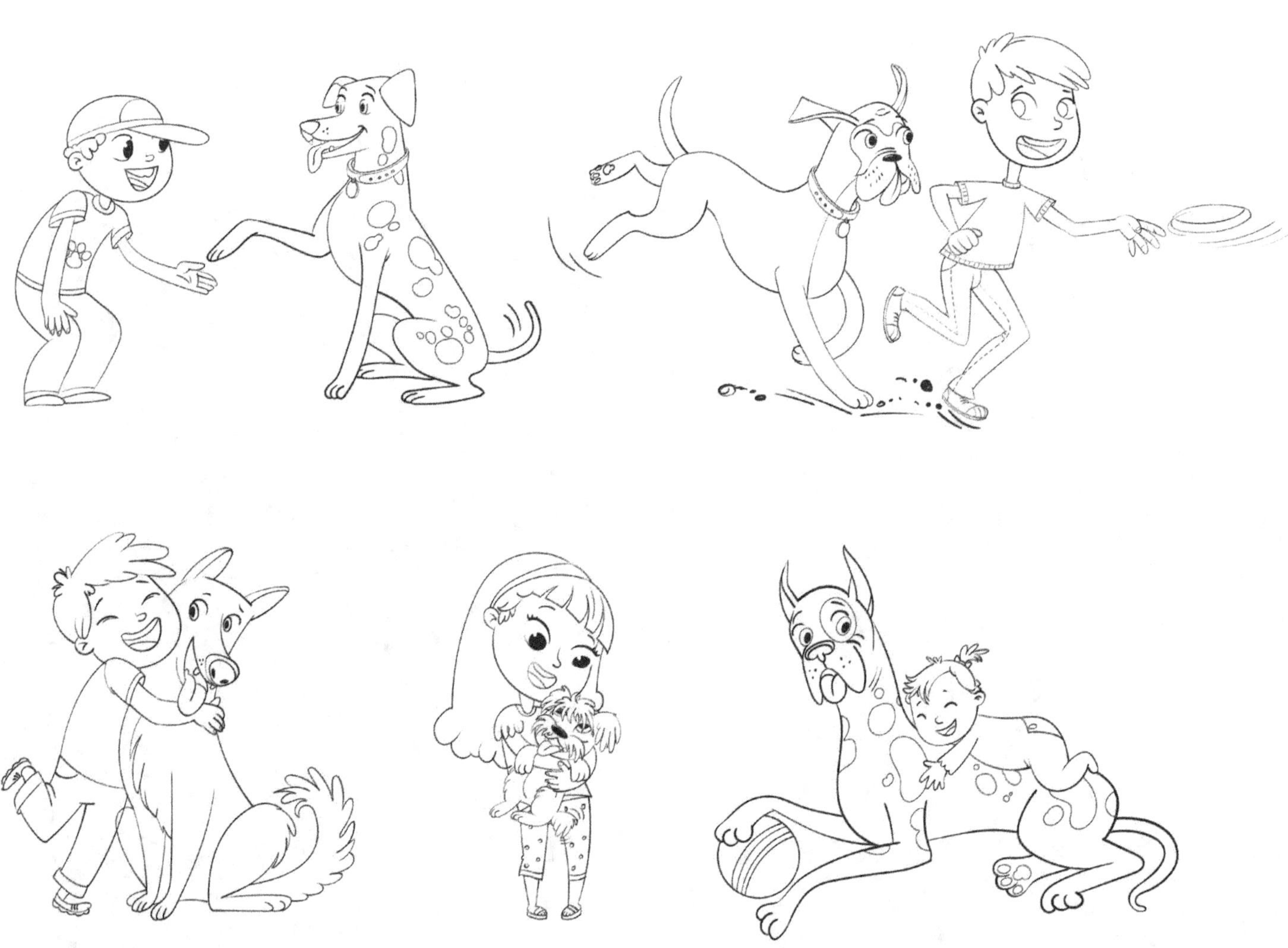

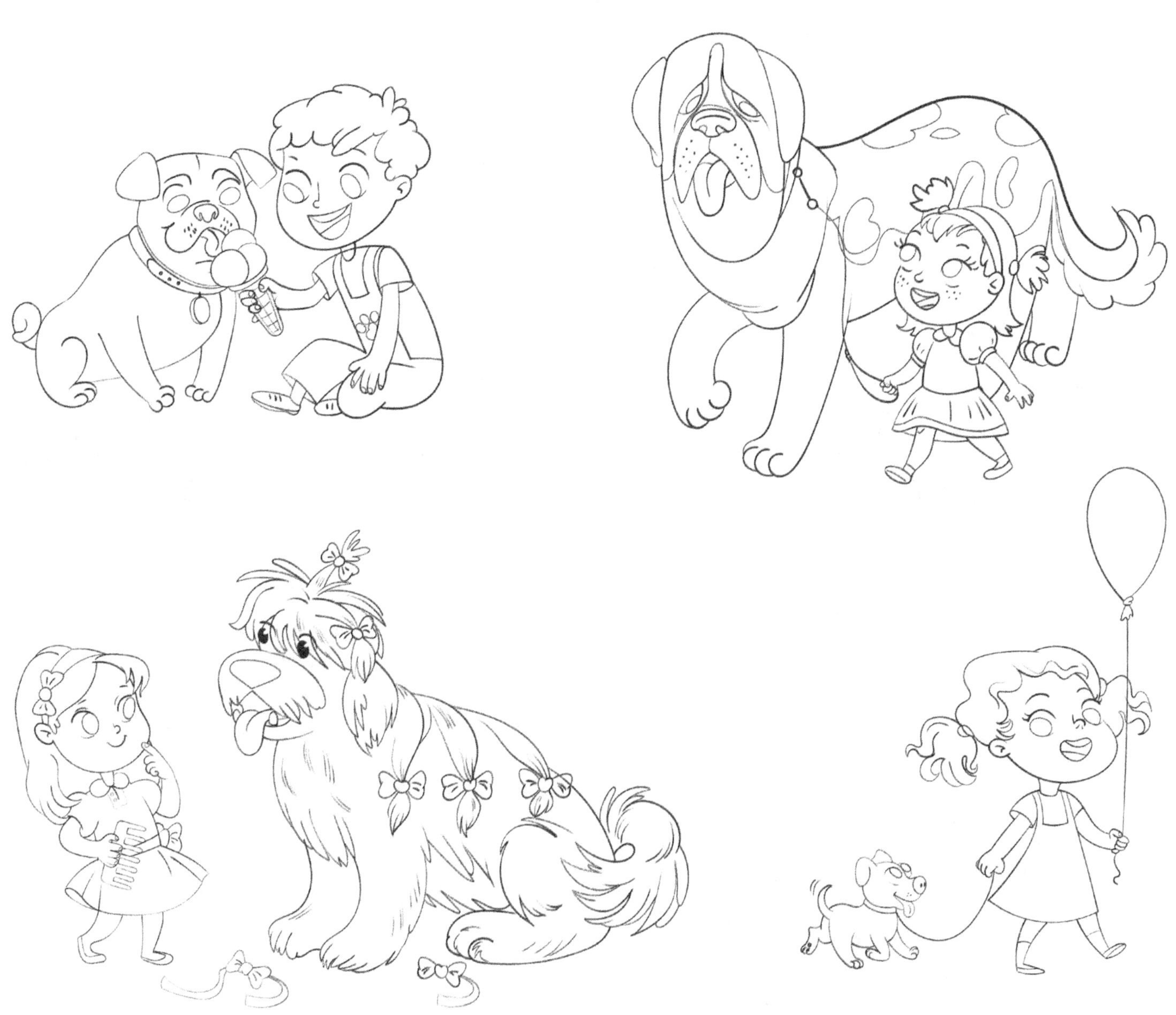

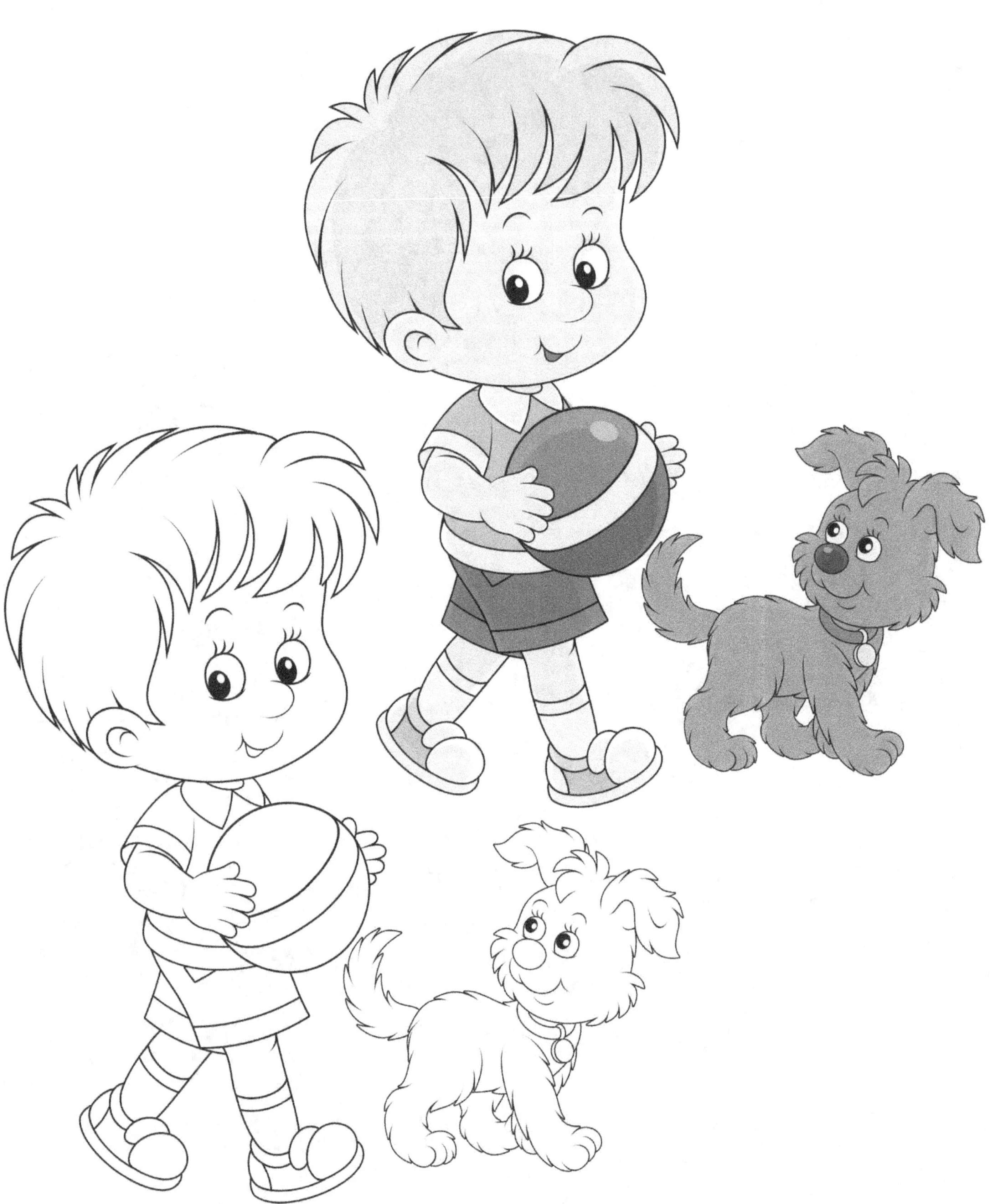

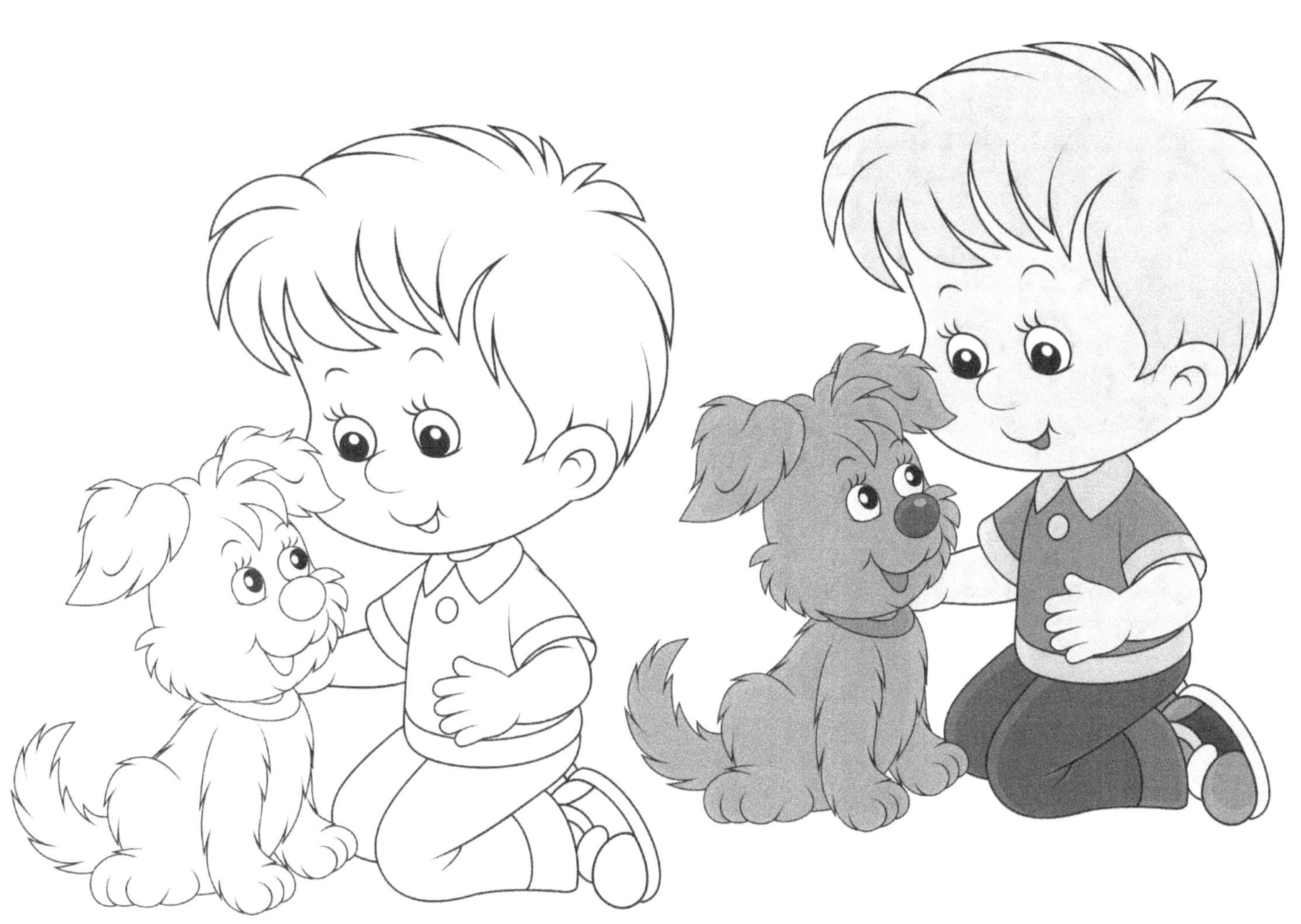

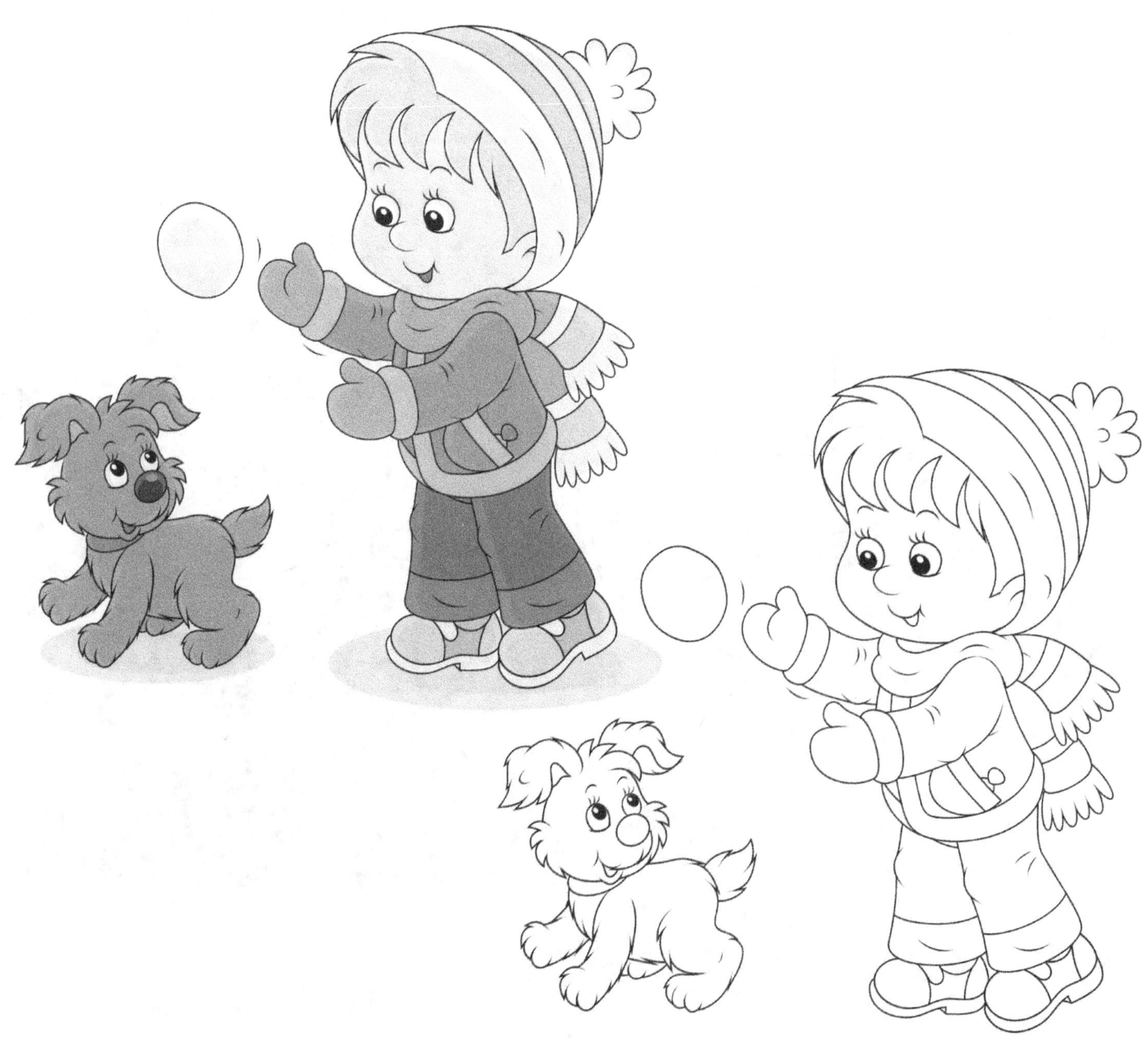

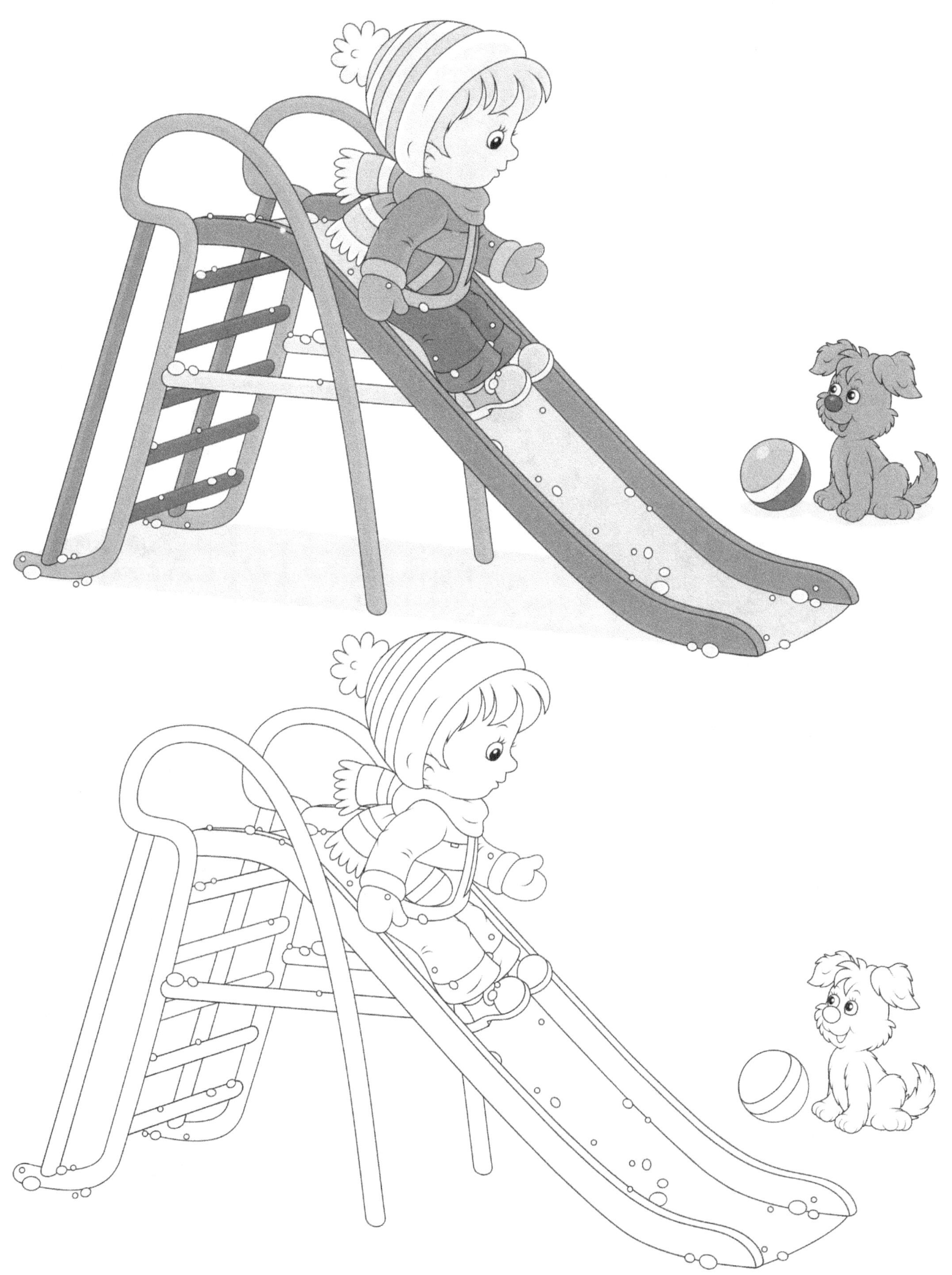

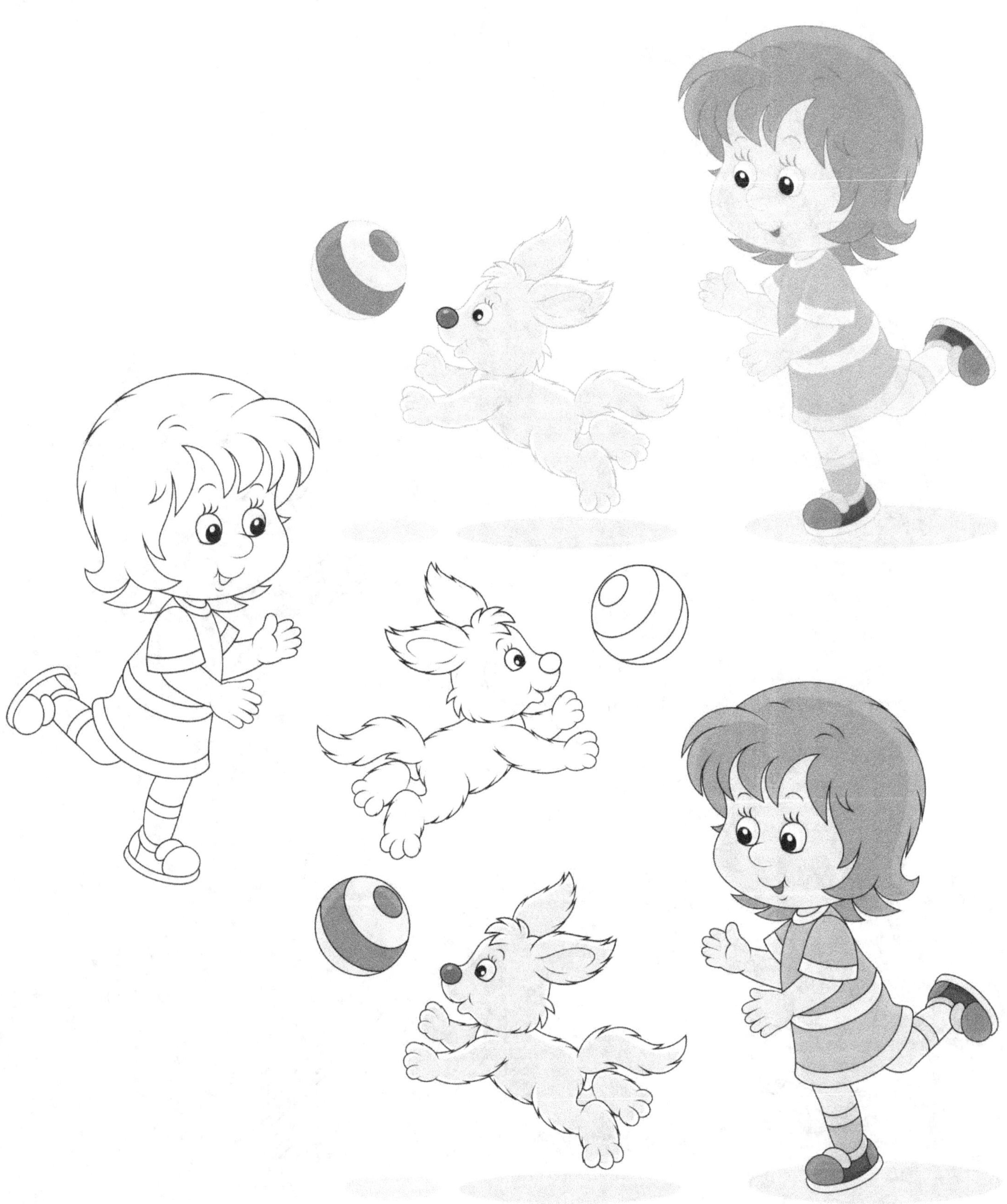

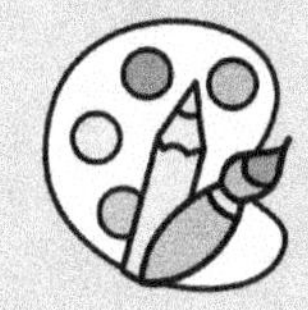
COLORING BOOK
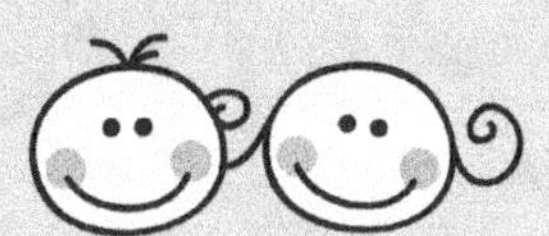

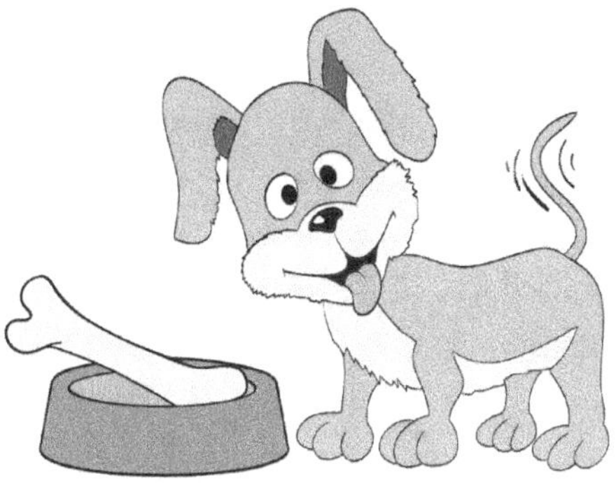

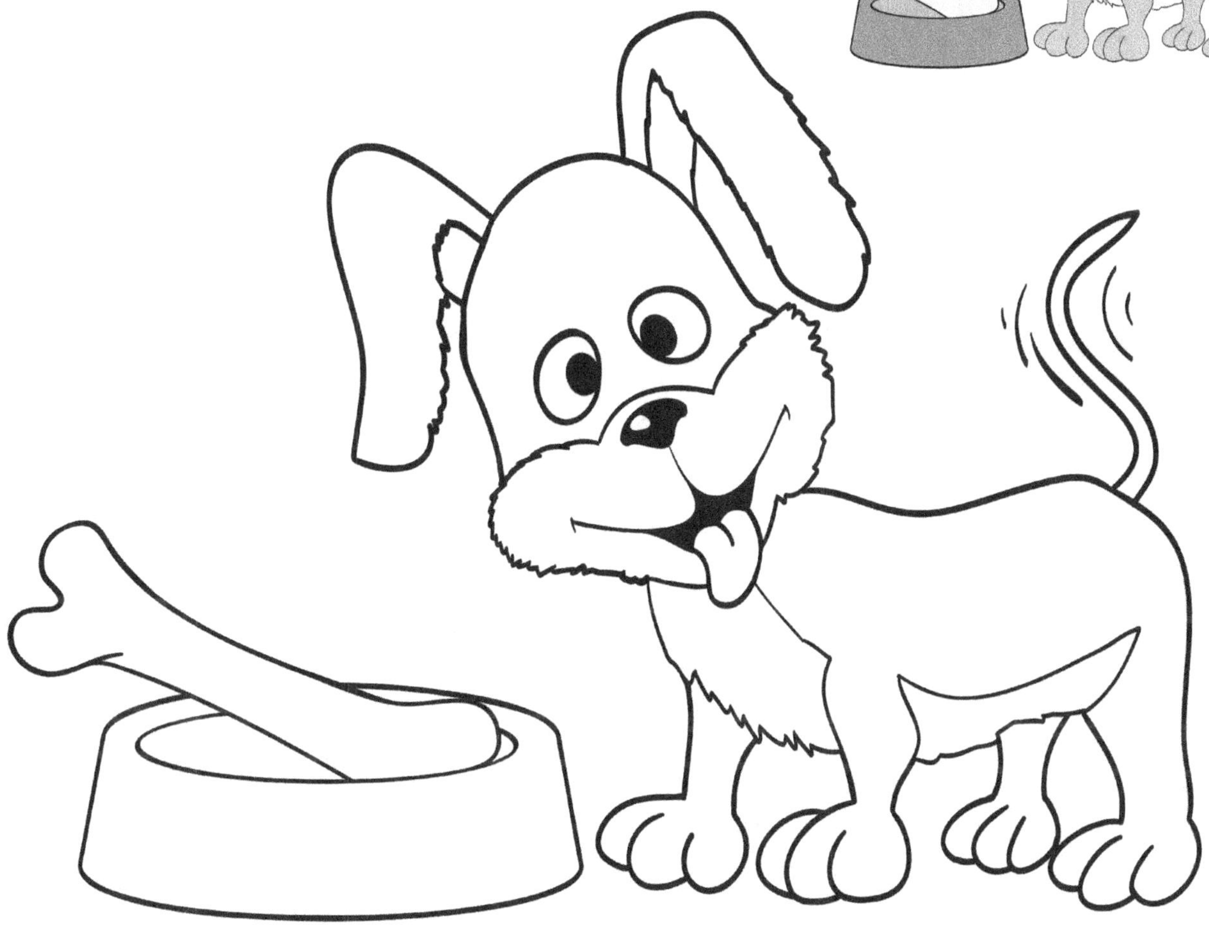